W9-AMU-978

Radiant Star Quilts

Eleanor Burns

Lenore Ryden
Amie Potter
48" x 48"

For my Grandchildren, Jonas, Kylee and Ellie

The three grandchildren are certainly my bright little stars! Delightful Ellie is the oldest, and my namesake. Hopefully, she will be an espiring quilter. Ellie and brother Jonas, our endearing boy, are children to Grant and Jimna. Sweet Kylee, the newest addition to the Burns' family, is the daughter of Orion and Teresa. Without a doubt, they are the joy of my life!

Cover Quilt: Pastel Splendor

Featuring Eleanor's newest fabric line Perennials, Pastel Splendor is elegant and fresh with four small Stars pieced into background corners. Amie quilted a dense pattern in the background and a double leaf pattern in the main Star.

Eleanor Burns
Amie Potter
70" x 70"

First Edition
May 1990
Second Edition
January, 2011
Published by Quilt in a Day®, Inc.
1955 Diamond Street, San Marcos, CA 92078
©2011 by Eleanor A. Burns Family Trust

ISBN 1-891776-52-5

Art Director: Merritt Voigtlander
Production Artist: Marie Harper

Printed in China. All rights reserved. No part of this material may be reproduced in any form or by any electronic or mechanical means, including information storage and retrieval systems, without permission in writing from the author. The publisher presents the information in this book in good faith. No warranty is given, nor are results guaranteed.

Contents

Introduction

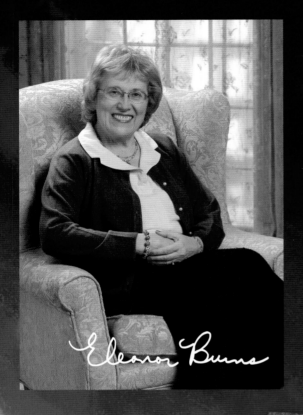

Eleanor Burns

The Radiant Star, also known as the Lone Star, Texas Star, and Star of Bethlehem, has long been a favorite among quilt lovers. In this dramatic design, one large multi-pieced star covers the mattress top from side to side. The star appears to burst from the center and radiate to the tips of the eight large identical diamonds. With carefully selected colors, the quilt virtually appears to pulsate or explode from the radiant color outward.

Valerie Sullivan taught me how to make my first Radiant Star Wallhanging on a gorgeous day in May of 1985. The days that Valerie and I quilted together were always bright… full of laughter and a lively exchange of ideas and techniques. I glowed over that first wallhanging with its perfectly matched center and finished in only seven hours!

With Valerie's expertise, Quilt in a Day published its first fold out pattern on the Four Color Radiant Star Wallhanging in 1986. Soon after, Jan Donner cleverly added two more colors to the star, and the Six Color Wallhanging was born.

Twenty-five years later, the new additions are impressive! The exclusive Quilt in a Day's Bias Stripper helps cut perfect Diamonds in a jiffy, plus it doubles as a tool for cutting bias binding. The Set In Triangle Ruler is extra large, and versatile for cutting Diamond strips, squaring completed Diamonds, and cutting Side triangles. Look forward to a new cutting adventure!

4

There are six different sizes of Radiant Stars from Wallhanging to queen, plus a seven color larger sized Star just perfect for King size quilts. All quilts are strip pieced, with techniques to help avoid the dreaded "volcano" in the center.

Solid Squares and Triangles

The Radiant Star on the left is a traditional version strip pieced with six fabrics, and finished with solid pieces of Background Corners and Side Triangles. Extensive charts take the math out of sizes for Corners and Triangles.

Superstitions relating to the Radiant Star quilt once circulated, including if a single girl made one she would never marry.

Optional Stripe for Corners and Side Triangles

Corners and Side Triangles are now more adventurous! In the quilt on the right, Corners and Side Triangles are jazzed up with a new finish of mitered stripes. Pick out your coordinating stripe when selecting your Radiant Star fabrics and Background. Yardage is included for each size quilt.

Optional Little Stars for Corners

For another optional finish for Corners, add stunning Little Stars, strip pieced and bias cut with no inset pieces. Purchase extra fabric for Little Stars when selecting your Radiant Star fabrics and Background. Yardage is included for each size quilt.

The new techniques found in *Radiant Star Quilts* are revolutionary. Radiate warmth in your home. Make quilts for all your stars.

Fabric Selection

Carol pays tribute to the most important battle of the Civil War in this striking version of six color Radiant Star. She separated background fabric lengths with leftover diamond strips and added a fourth border. Judy quilted swirly feathers in the cream background with loops and scallop variations in the borders and Star.

Star of Gettysburg
Carol Frey
Judy Jackson
90" x 106"

Select one **multicolored fabric in 100% cotton as your inspiration piece**. From that fabric, choose additional fabrics with similar weight and weave in combinations of light, medium, and dark values for a dynamic radiating effect from the center outward.

To avoid a "choppy look" in the Star, select fabrics with a **gradual color value**. In addition, vary the scales of your prints. Choose a mix of large scale prints, small scale prints, and ones that look like solids from a distance.

Choose a bright or contrasting color for your Radiant to emphasize its circular position in the Star. A large scale print also draws attention to the Radiant. The Yardage Charts list each Radiant position for the various projects. Same color fabrics are repeated on both sides of the Radiant to further boost its emphasis.

Fabric A is always positioned in the center of the Star, as well as the outer most points. Since the center point is a challenge to match, avoid solid colored fabric that maximizes imperfect match points. Dark colored print fabric is a better choice as recommended in the Yardage Charts. A light fabric used in the center appears as a "hole" in the finished Star.

Avoid stripes and directional prints in the star. Stripes cut lengthwise do not have the same give as those fabrics cut from selvage to selvage. However, stripes are dynamic in a border.

For Background, solid fabric or one that appears solid from a distance is best. It's helpful to choose **Background** fabric after the Star is completed. This way, the Star can be laid out on several choices and "interviewed". Background fabric should not be similar to the Radiant or Fabric A for the Star to shine. The Star appears to sparkle in a clear night sky when placed on a dark background variation.

Backing Fabric

Choose light backing fabric and thin batting if you plan to finish your Radiant Star with machine quilting. If you use light Background for corners and triangles, avoid a dark backing because it shows through.

Batting

Select an 80/20 blend (80% cotton and 20% polyester) or 100% cotton batting for your quilt. A thin batting, 2 or 3 oz, is best and can be either hand or machine quilted.

Supplies

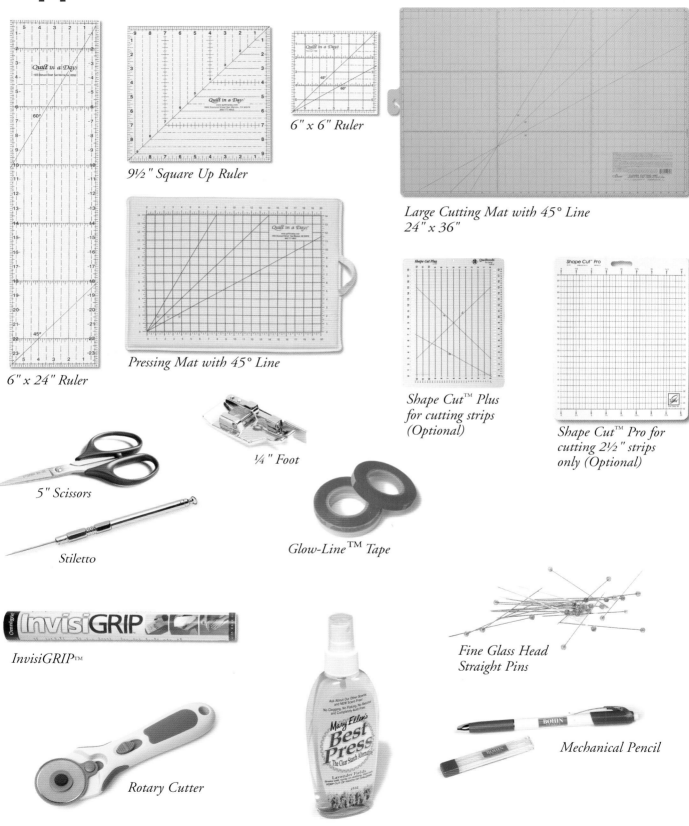

6" x 24" Ruler

9½" Square Up Ruler

6" x 6" Ruler

Large Cutting Mat with 45° Line
24" x 36"

Pressing Mat with 45° Line

Shape Cut™ Plus
for cutting strips
(Optional)

Shape Cut™ Pro for
cutting 2½" strips
only (Optional)

5" Scissors

¼" Foot

Stiletto

Glow-Line™ Tape

Fine Glass Head
Straight Pins

InvisiGRIP™

Rotary Cutter

Mary Ellen's Best Press

Mechanical Pencil

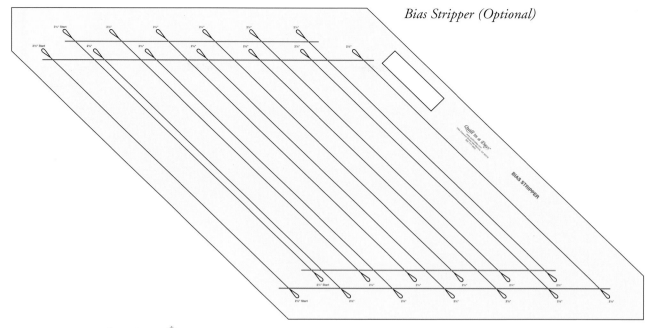

Bias Stripper (Optional)

Set In Triangle Ruler
(Optional)

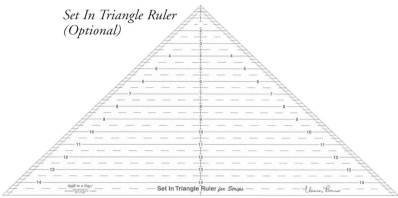

Supplies for Machine Quilting on Conventional Sewing Machine

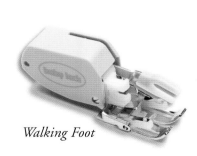

Walking Foot

Darning Foot

Stencil for
Free Motion Quilting

Safety Pins with Pin Covers

Quilt Clamps

Kwik Klip

Radiant Star Yardage
Four Color Wallhanging

Burst of Glory
Angela Castro
Judy Jackson
50" x 50"

Lady Liberty would be proud. Angela's four color Star Wallhanging bursts like a firecracker in the summer sky. A continuous line motif is quilted in bold, contrasting red thread in the dark blue background. Double loops provide a nice texture inside the Star and also in the outside border.

Make a sample paste up Diamond on page 23.

Follow the Four Color Star sewing instructions beginning on page 30.

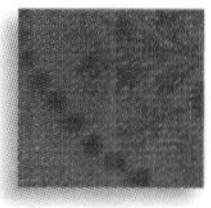

A 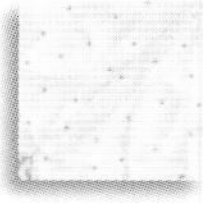   B    C 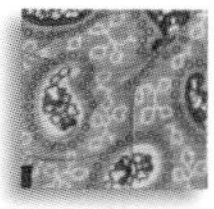   D

Four Color Wallhanging	50" x 50"
Fabric A Dark	**¼ yd**
Center and Star Points	(2) 2½" strips
Fabric B Light	**⅜ yd**
Diamonds	(4) 2½" strips
Fabric C Medium	**⅝ yd**
Diamonds	(6) 2½" strips
Fabric D Dark	**⅜ yd**
Radiant Diamonds	(4) 2½" strips
Background	**1⅜ yds**
Solid Squares and Triangles	Cut later
First Border	**⅜ yd**
	(4) 2½" strips
Second Border	**¾ yd**
	(5) 5" strips
Binding	½ yd
	(5) 3" strips
Backing	3 yds
Batting	60" x 60"

Optional 10" Little Stars for Corners   Page 80

Fabric A	**⅛ yd**
Center	(2) 1½" strips
Fabric B	**¼ yd**
Radiant	(4) 1½" strips
Fabric C	**⅛ yd**
Star Points	(2) 1½" strips
Background	**Yardage included in chart on left**
	(2) 4¼" strips cut into (16) 4¼" squares
	(2) 3½" strips cut into (16) 3½" squares
	(6) 1½" strips

Optional Stripe for Corners and Side Triangles
Page 66

Stripe Fabric	**1 yd**
Stripes	Approximately 4½" wide
Background	**Yardage included in chart on left**

Four Color Lap

Emerald and Amethyst
Teresa Varnes
Judy Jackson
55" x 64"

Teresa chose rich purples and decadent greens for her Wallhanging. A light purple Background magnifies her glittering Star. Judy quilted loops to enhance the Star and swirly feathers that seem to dance in a sparkling circle around the Star.

Make a sample paste up Diamond on page 23.

Follow the Four Color Star sewing instructions beginning on page 30.

A   B   C   D

Four Color Lap	55" x 64"
Fabric A Dark	**¼ yd**
Center and Star Points	(2) 2½" strips
Fabric B Light	**⅜ yd**
Diamonds	(4) 2½" strips
Fabric C Medium	**⅝ yd**
Diamonds	(6) 2½" strips
Fabric D Dark	**⅜ yd**
Radiant Diamonds	(4) 2½" strips
Background	**1¾ yds**
Sides	(2) 1½" strips
Top and Bottom	(2) 6" strips
Solid Squares and Triangles	Cut later
First Border	**⅜ yd**
	(5) 2½" strips
Second Border	**1⅛ yds**
	(6) 6" strips
Binding	⅔ yd
	(7) 3" strips
Backing	3¾ yds
Batting	65" x 74"

Optional 10" Little Stars for Corners	Page 80
Fabric A	**⅛ yd**
Center	(2) 1½" strips
Fabric B	**¼ yd**
Radiant	(4) 1½" strips
Fabric C	**⅛ yd**
Star Points	(2) 1½" strips
Background	**Yardage included in chart on left**
	(2) 4¼" strips cut into (16) 4¼" squares
	(2) 3½" strips cut into (16) 3½" squares
	(6) 1½" strips

Optional Stripe for Corners and Side Triangles	Page 66
Stripe Fabric	**1 yd**
Stripes	Approximately 4½" wide
Background	**Yardage included in chart on left**

Four Color Twin

Sunny Skies
Sue Bouchard
Amie Potter
64" x 87"

Vibrant yellows and luscious oranges flash off this quilt like rays from the sun. Sue's twin size quilt is the ideal showpiece for a child's bedroom. The four-color Star is quilted with a stylized leaf, which is repeated in the yellow border. Loops meander around all the other borders. Amie filled the large open areas with two different styles of crosshatching, setting off the Star to perfection.

Make a sample paste up Diamond on page 23.

Follow the Four Color Star sewing instructions beginning on page 30.

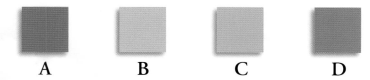

A   B   C   D

Four Color Twin	64" x 88"
Fabric A Dark	**¼ yd**
Center and Star Points	(2) 2½" strips
Fabric B Light .	**⅜ yd**
Diamonds	(4) 2½" strips
Fabric C Medium	**⅝ yd**
Diamonds	(6) 2½" strips
Fabric D Dark	**⅜ yd**
Radiant Diamonds	(4) 2½" strips
Background	**2 yds**
Top and Bottom	(2) 10½" strips
Solid Squares and Triangles	Cut later
First Border	**¾ yd**
	(6) 2½" strips
Second Border	**1¼ yds**
	(7) 5" strips
Third Border	**1⅞ yds**
	(8) 7½" strips
Binding	⅞ yd
	(8) 3" strips
Backing	5½ yds
Batting	74" x 98"

Optional 10" Little Stars for Corners   Page 80

Fabric A	**⅛ yd**
Center	(2) 1½" strips
Fabric B	**¼ yd**
Radiant	(4) 1½" strips
Fabric C	**⅛ yd**
Star Points	(2) 1½" strips
Background	**Yardage included in chart on left**
	(2) 4¼" strips cut into (16) 4¼" squares
	(2) 3½" strips cut into (16) 3½" squares
	(6) 1½" strips

Optional Stripe for Corners and Side Triangles
                                           Page 66

Stripe Fabric	**1 yd**
Stripes	Approximately 4½" wide
Background	**Yardage included in chart on left**

Six Color Wallhanging

Chocolate Mint
Robin Kinley
66" x 66"

A border fabric jingling with bells, ornaments, snowflakes and stars gave Robin the inspiration to select the rest of her Christmas fabric. Tones of mint, deep cherry red, and chocolate brown make her quilt good enough to eat. She used continuous curve quilting in the Star. Robin marked three circles to use as registration lines and freehanded the feather circles and half circles. Using tight vertical loops around the feathers made the feathers "pop."

Make a sample paste up Diamond on page 24.

Follow the Six Color Star sewing instructions beginning on page 34.

Six Color Wallhanging	66" x 66"
Fabric A Dark	**¼ yd**
Center and Star Points	(2) 2½" strips
Fabric B Medium	**⅜ yd**
Diamonds	(4) 2½" strips
Fabric C Light	**⅝ yd**
Diamonds	(6) 2½" strips
Fabric D Medium	**¾ yd**
Diamonds	(8) 2½" strips
Fabric E Medium	**⅞ yd**
Diamonds	(10) 2½" strips
Fabric F Dark	**⅝ yd**
Radiant Diamonds	(6) 2½" strips
Background	**2 yds**
Solid Squares and Triangles	Cut later
First Border	**½ yd**
	(6) 2" strips
Second Border	**1¼ yds**
	(7) 5½" strips
Binding	⅞ yd
	(8) 3" strips
Backing	4¼ yds
Batting	76" x 76"

Optional 10" Little Stars for Corners	Page 80
Fabric A	**⅛ yd**
Center	(2) 1½" strips
Fabric B	**¼ yd**
Radiant	(4) 1½" strips
Fabric C	**⅛ yd**
Star Points	(2) 1½" strips
Background	**Yardage included in chart on left**
	(2) 4¼" strips cut into (16) 4¼" squares
	(2) 3½" strips cut into (16) 3½" squares
	(2) 10½" strips cut into (8) 10½" squares

Optional Stripe for Corners and Side Triangles
Page 66

Stripe Fabric	2 yds
Stripes	Approximately 7½" wide
Background	**Yardage included in chart on left**

Six Color Queen

Garden Party
Julie Ferrick
Amie Potter
85" x 102"

Radiant Star is perfect to show off all the fabrics in Eleanor's "True Blue" fabric line. Greens, blues, and yellows mingle, making Julie's quilt luscious. Garden Party is festooned with feathers in a variety of styles in each background area and all borders. Simple quilted wavy lines set off the Star to perfection.

Make a sample paste up Diamond on page 24.

Follow the Six Color Star sewing instructions beginning on page 34.

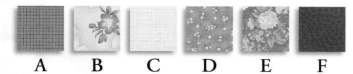

A B C D E F

Six Color Queen	85" x 102"
Fabric A Dark	¼ yd
Center and Star Points	(2) 2½" strips
Fabric B Medium	⅜ yd
Diamonds	(4) 2½" strips
Fabric C Light	⅝ yd
Diamonds	(6) 2½" strips
Fabric D Medium	¾ yd
Diamonds	(8) 2½" strips
Fabric E Medium	⅞ yd
Diamonds	(10) 2½" strips
Fabric F Dark	⅝ yd
Radiant Diamonds	(6) 2½" strips
Background	2½ yds
Top and Bottom	(3) 6½" strips
Solid Squares and Triangles	Cut later
First Border	¾ yd
	(7) 3½" strips
Second Border	1⅓ yds
	(8) 5½" strips
Third Border	2 yds
	(9) 7½" strips
Binding	1 yd
	(9) 3" strips
Backing	7¾ yds
Batting	95" x 112"

Optional 10" Little Stars for Corners	Page 80
Fabric A	⅛ yd
Center	(2) 1½" strips
Fabric B	¼ yd
Radiant	(4) 1½" strips
Fabric C	⅛ yd
Star Points	(2) 1½" strips
Background	**Yardage included in chart on left**
	(2) 4¼" strips cut into (16) 4¼" squares
	(2) 3½" strips cut into (16) 3½" squares
	(2) 10½" strips cut into (8) 10½" squares

Optional Stripe for Corners and Side Triangles
Page 66

Stripe Fabric	2 yds
Stripes	Approximately 7½" wide
Background	**Yardage included in chart on left**

Seven Color King

Caribbean Star
Karyn Helsel
Amie Potter
106" x 106"

Karyn has a dream to go to the Caribbean so what better way to make a nightly sojourn to the tranquil waters than with these teal blue hues used in her quilt. An allover quilt pattern with frolicking fish, dolphins, sea horses and turtles capture the essence of the sea. Swirls that suggest waves finish the outside border. Sweet dreams, Karyn and Norman!

Make a sample paste up Diamond on page 25.

Follow the Seven Color Star sewing instructions beginning on page 38.

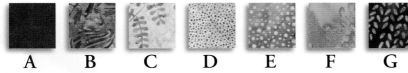

A B C D E F G

Seven Color King	106" x 106"
Fabric A Dark	**¼ yd**
Center and Star Points	(2) 2½" strips
Fabric B Medium .	**⅜ yd**
Diamonds	(4) 2½" strips
Fabric C Light	**⅝ yd**
Diamonds	(6) 2½" strips
Fabric D Medium	**¾ yd**
Diamonds	(8) 2½" strips
Fabric E Medium	**⅞ yd**
Diamonds	(10) 2½" strips
Fabric F Medium	**1 yd**
Diamonds	(12) 2½" strips
Fabric G Dark	**⅝ yds**
Radiant Diamonds	(7) 2½" strips
Background	**3¾ yds**
First Border	(8) 6" strips
Solid Squares and Triangles	Cut later
Second Border	**1 yd**
	(8) 3½" strips
Third Border	**1⅝ yds**
	(9) 5½" strips
Fourth Border	**2¼ yds**
	(10) 7½" strips
Binding	1⅛ yds
	(11) 3" strips
Backing	9½ yds
Batting	116" x 116"

Optional 10" Little Stars for Corners	Page 80
Fabric A	**¼ yd**
Center	(4) 2" strips
Fabric B	**⅝ yd**
Radiant	(8) 2" strips
Fabric C	**¼ yd**
Star Points	(4) 2" strips
Background	**Yardage included in chart on left**
	(2) 5½" strips cut into (16) 5½" squares
	(2) 4½" strips cut into (16) 4½" squares
	(8) 3½" strips

Optional Stripe for Corners and Side Triangles	Page 66
Stripe Fabric	**2½ yds**
Stripes	Approximately 9½" wide
Background	**Yardage included in chart on left**

Paste Up Pages

Visualize how your finished Star will look in a few easy steps.

1. **Four Color Radiant Stars:** Cut one ¾" strip from each of your fabrics.

2. **Six Color Radiant Stars:** Cut one ⅝" strip from each of your fabrics.

3. **Seven Color Radiant Stars:** Cut one ½" strip from each of your fabrics.

4. Photo copy appropriate paste up sheet.

5. Trace appropriate size template on template plastic and cut out. Tape to edge of small rule for rotary cutting.

6. Layer strips.

7. Cut strips on 45° angle into diamonds.

8. Paste Diamond in place with a glue stick.

9. **Optional:** Make eight color copies, cut out diamond shapes and tape together into a Star for a preview of your finished quilt.

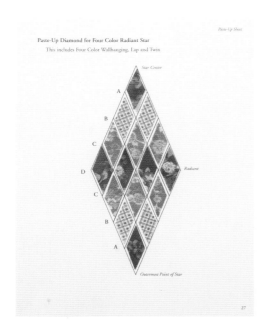

Paste-Up Diamond for Four Color Radiant Star

This includes Four Color Wallhanging, Lap and Twin.

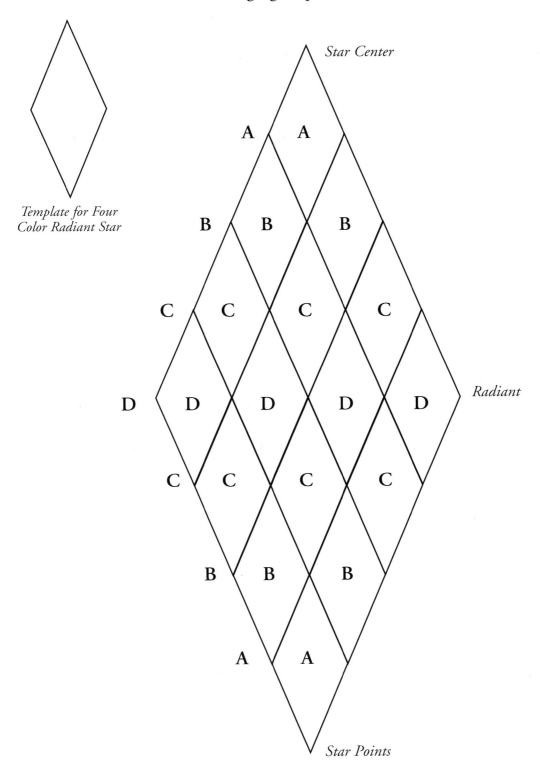

Template for Four Color Radiant Star

*This is the ONLY page you may photocopy.

Paste-Up Diamond for Six Color Radiant Star

This includes Six Color
Wallhanging and Queen.

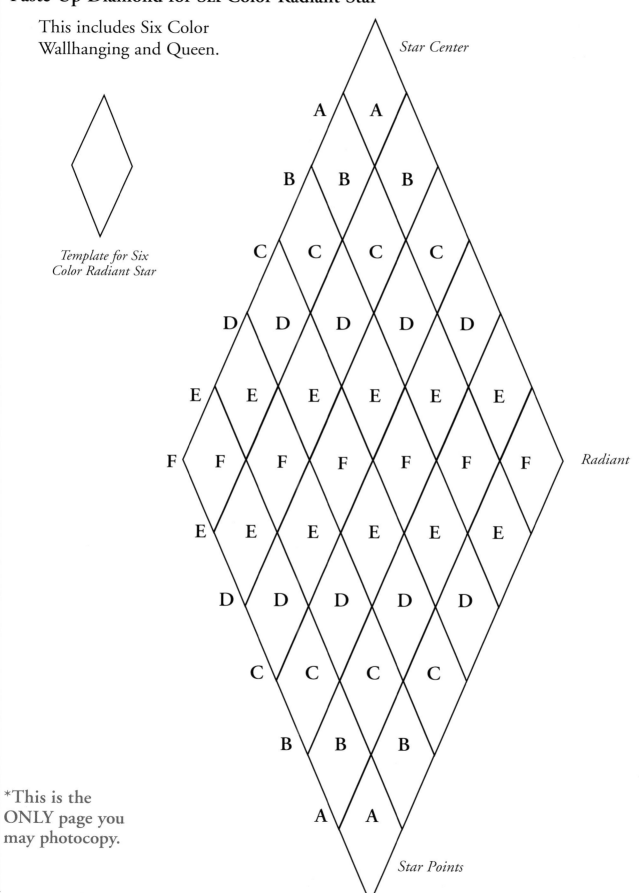

*Template for Six
Color Radiant Star*

Star Center

Radiant

Star Points

*This is the
ONLY page you
may photocopy.

Paste-Up Diamond for Seven Color Radiant Star

This is for King.

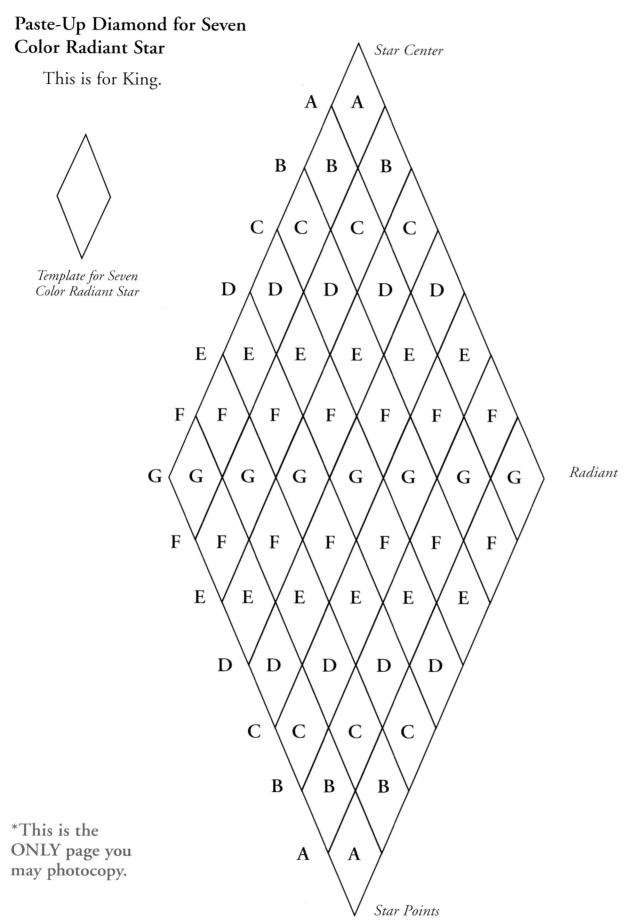

Template for Seven Color Radiant Star

Star Center

Radiant

Star Points

*This is the ONLY page you may photocopy.

Cutting Strips

There are three different rulers suggested for cutting your 2½" strips.
Select one of them: 6" x 24" Ruler
        Shape Cut Plus
        Shape Cut Pro

Cutting Strips with 6" x 24" Ruler and Cutter

Use a large rotary cutter with a 6" x 24" ruler marked with a 45° line and 18" x 24" or 24" x 36" cutting mat, also marked with a 45° line. Put Invisigrip on bottom side of ruler so ruler does not slip when cutting. If fabric is light weight, spray with spray starch.

1. Press fabric and fold in half, matching selvage edges.

2. Place fabric on cutting mat with folded edge along horizontal line, and straight edge on vertical line.

3. Place ½" line on ruler on left vertical edge of fabric.

4. Spread your fingers and place four on top of ruler with little finger on mat to keep ruler firmly in place.

5. Take rotary cutter in your free hand and open blade. Starting below fabric, begin cutting away from you, applying pressure on ruler and cutter. Keeping blade next to ruler's edge, straighten edge of fabric.

6. Cut 2½" strips for blocks. To help you, place Glow-Line™ Tape from Omnigrid® to left of 2½" line on bottom side. Open first strip and look at fold to see if it is straight. If fabric is crooked, repeat preceding steps.

7. Suggested widths for Borders are given, but can be changed as long as you get the size quilt you desire.

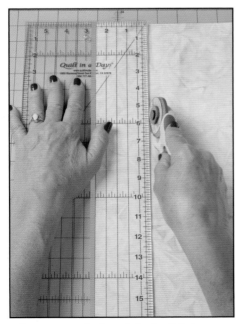

If you are right-handed, the fabric should trail off to the right.

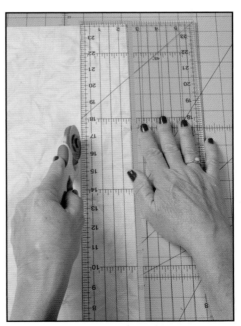

If you are left-handed, the fabric should trail off to the left.

Cutting Strips with Shape Cut™

Select between two different Shape Cut rulers:

- Shape Cut Plus
- Shape Cut Pro

Layer Cutting Strips with Shape Cut Plus

*The Shape Cut Plus is a 12" x 18" slotted ruler for cutting **fabric folded in fourths** into selvage to selvage strips at ½" increments.*

1. Place Glow-Line™ Tape at 2½" measurements.

2. **Fold fabric into fourths,** lining up fold with selvage edges.

3. Place Shape Cut Plus on fabric. Line up zero horizontal line with bottom edge of fabric. Allow extra fabric to left of zero vertical line for straightening.

4. Place blade of cutter in zero slot, and straighten left edge of fabric. Cut strips at 2½" for Star.

5. Cut Borders according to Yardage Charts.

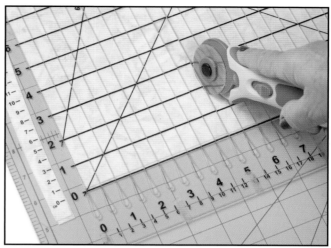

Line up zero horizontal line with bottom edge of fabric. Place rotary blade in 2½" slots and cut.

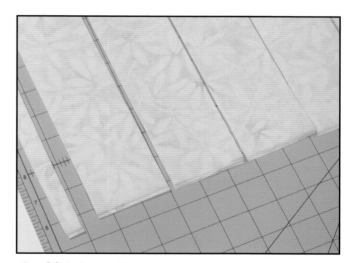

Cut fabric into strips.

Layer Cutting Strips with Shape Cut Pro

*The Shape Cut Pro is a large 20" x 23" slotted ruler for cutting **folded 20"** widths of fabric into 2½" selvage to selvage strips.*

1. Stack Fabric B and then Fabric A on cutting mat, lining up left and selvage edges with zero horizontal line on mat.

2. Place Shape Cut Pro on fabric. Line up zero horizontal line with bottom edge of fabric. Allow extra fabric to left of vertical zero for straightening.

3. Place blade of cutter in zero slot, and straighten left edge of fabric.

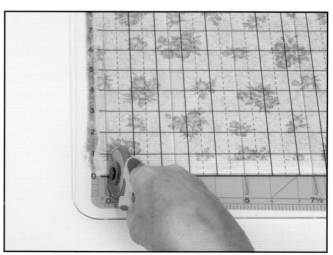

Place blade of cutter in zero slot, and straighten left edge of fabric.

4. Cut strips for Diamonds at 2½" according to Yardage and Cutting Charts.

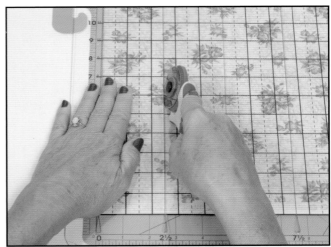

Place cutter in slots, and cut 2½" strips.

5. Cut Fabric A until you have enough for your particular size quilt. Continue cutting Fabric B strips

Cut all Fabric A strips.

6. Stack strips.

7. Repeat layering and cutting 2½" Fabric D and Fabric C strips for Diamonds. Continue until all 2½" strips are cut.

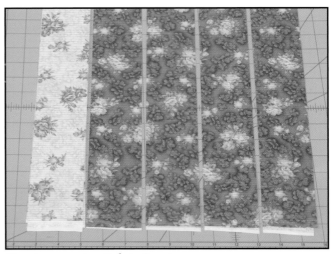

Continue cutting Fabric B strips.

Stitches Per Inch and Seam Allowance

Stitches Per Inch

Place a fine, sharp #70/10 needle on your machine. Set machine at 15 stitches per inch, or 2.0 on computerized machines. Thread your machine with a good quality neutral shade polyester or cotton spun thread.

Seam Allowance

Sew an accurate and consistent ¼" seam allowance.

Place a ¼" foot on sewing machine.

¼" Foot

Cut three 1½" x 6" pieces of fabric.

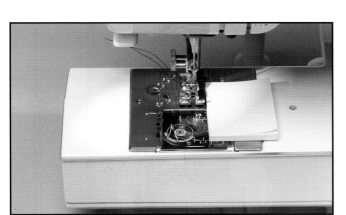

If a ¼" foot is not available, place some Post-It® notes ¼" from needle for a seam guide.

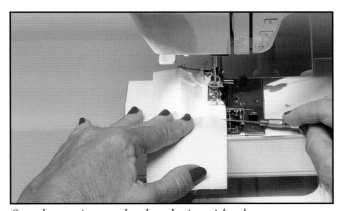

Sew three strips together lengthwise with what you think is a ¼" seam.

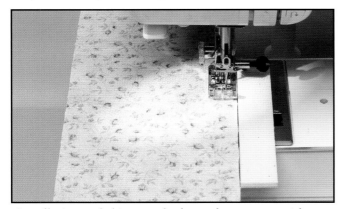

An adhesive moleskin can also be used as a seam guide.

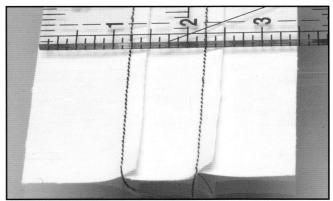

Press seams in one direction and measure. Width should be 3½". If sample measures smaller than 3½", seam is too large. If seam measures larger than 3½", seam is too small.

Four Color Radiant Star

Teresa Varnes
Amie Potter
50" x 50"

A   **B**   **C**   **D**

The key shows the position of each fabric in the quilt, and how strips are sewn together.

Making Section One for Four Color Star

1. Pencil in color names of your fabrics, or paste in small fabric swatches.

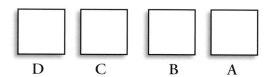

D C B A

2. Line up one 2½" strip of each fabric in this order. **Offset each strip 2".** **Work from right to left.**

3. Flip Fabric A to Fabric B, right sides together, lengthwise.

4. Sew ¼" seam with A on top, wrong side up, and B underneath, 2" down from top of A. Open.

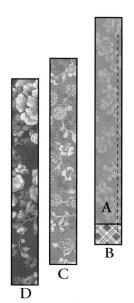

Do not pull on strips as you sew them together.

5. Place C to B, right sides together, and 2" down from the top. Sew with B on top, wrong side up. Open.

6. Sew on D in same offset order.

7. **Complete a second set of Section One.**

8. Press seams to one side **away from Fabric A** and label as Section One. See page 33.

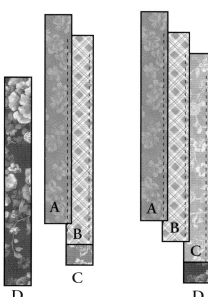

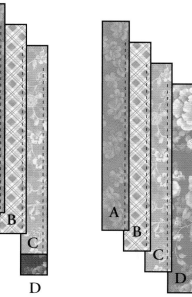

Press seams away from Fabric A.

Making Section Two for Four Color Star

1. Pencil in color names of your fabrics, or paste in small fabric swatches.

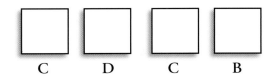

C   D   C   B

2. Line up one 2½" strip of each fabric. **Offset each strip 2". Work from right to left.**

3. Flip B to C, right sides together, lengthwise.

4. Sew with B on top, wrong side up, and C underneath, 2" down from top of B. Open.

5. Place D to C, right sides together, and 2" down from top. Sew with C on top, wrong side up. Open.

6. Sew C in same offset order.

7. **Complete a second set of Section Two.**

8. Press seams to one side **away from Fabric B** and label as Section Two.

9. Turn to **Cutting Diamond Strips** on page 43.

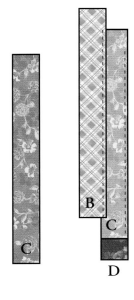

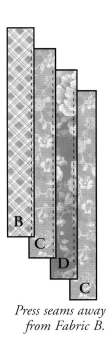

Press seams away from Fabric B.

Pressing Strips

*If fabric is light weight, press
with spray starch.*

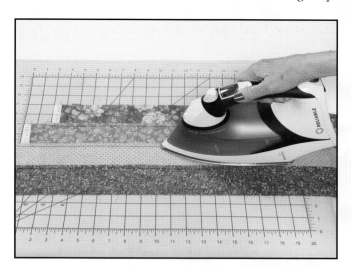

1. Place strips on padded pressing mat.
   Padding helps prevent seams showing
   from wrong side.

2. Press **across** strips rather than length of
   strips. Begin on wrong side first, and
   press seams to one side as directed.

3. Flip strips over and press on right side.
   Make sure there are no pleats at seam
   lines.

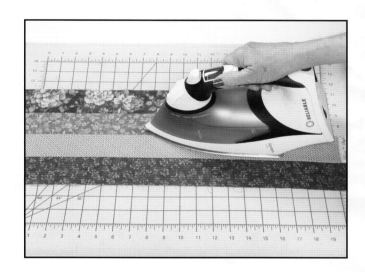

4. If your sewn together strips "bow"
   slightly when they are laid flat, you may
   have stretched them either when stitching or pressing. In that case, spray with
   water or starch and press again. Block
   them into straight lines as you press.

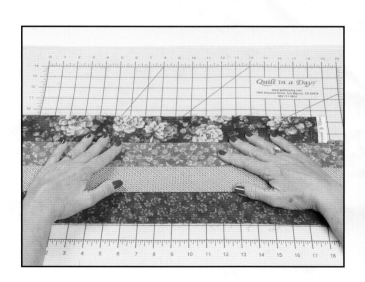

Six Color Radiant Star

Pastel Splendor
Eleanor Burns
Amie Potter
70" x 70"

A   B   C   D   E   F

The key shows the position of each fabric in the quilt, and how strips are sewn together.

Making Section One for Six Color Star

1. Pencil in color names of your fabrics, or paste in small fabric swatches.

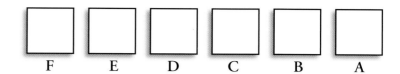

2. Line up one 2½" strip of each fabric in this order. Offset each strip 2". **Work from right to left.**

3. Flip Fabric A to Fabric B, right sides together, lengthwise.

4. Sew with A on top, wrong side up, and B underneath, 2" down from top of Fabric A. Open.

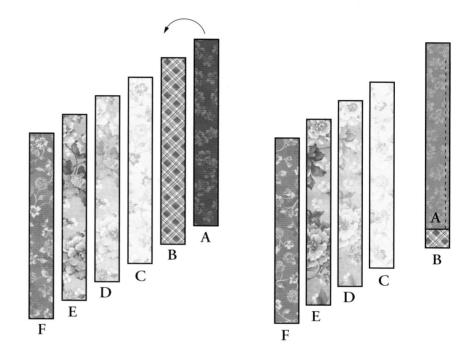

5. Sew on Fabric C, D, E and F in same offset order.

6. **Complete a second set of Section One.**

7. Press seams to one side **away from Fabric A** and label as Section One. See page 33.

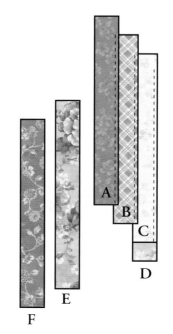

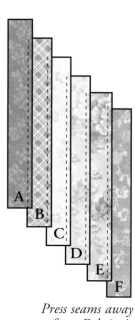

Press seams away from Fabric A.

Making Section Two for Six Color Star

1. Pencil in color names of your fabrics, or paste in small fabric swatches.

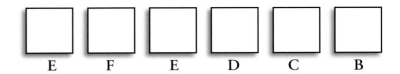

E F E D C B

2. Line up one 2½" strip of each fabric in this order. **Offset each strip 2". Work from right to left.**

3. Flip Fabric B to Fabric C, right sides together, lengthwise.

4. Sew with B on top, wrong side up, and C underneath, 2" down from top of B. Open.

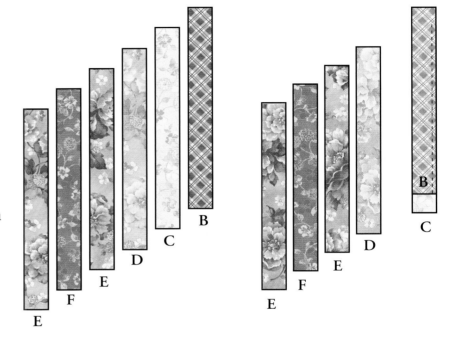

5. Sew on Fabrics D, E, F and E in same offset order.

6. **Complete a second set** of Section Two.

7. Carefully press seams to one side **away from Fabric B** and label as Section Two.

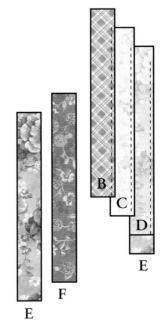

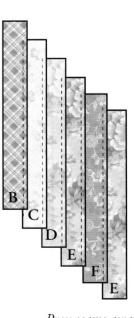

Press seams away from Fabric B.

Making Section Three for Six Color Star

1. Pencil in color names of your fabrics, or paste in small fabric swatches.

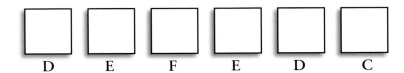

2. Line up one 2½" strip of each fabric in this order. **Offset each strip 2". Work from right to left.**

3. Flip Fabric C to Fabric D, right sides together, lengthwise.

4. Sew with C on top, wrong side up, and D underneath, 2" down from top of C. Open.

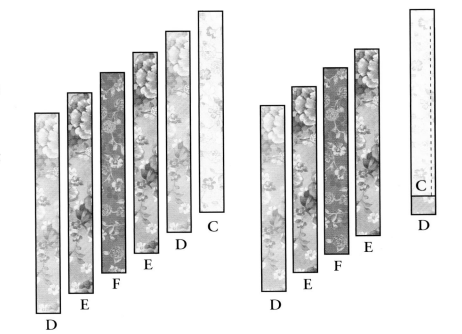

5. Sew on Fabric E, F, E and D in same offset order.

6. **Complete a second set** of Section Three.

7. Press seams to one side **away from Fabric C** and label as Section Three.

8. Turn to **Cutting Diamond Strips** on page 43.

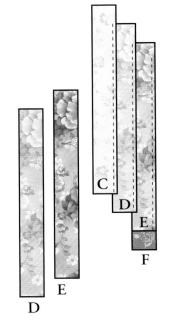

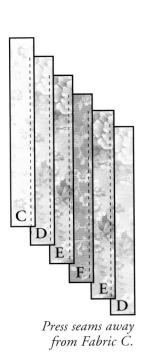

Press seams away from Fabric C.

Seven Color Radiant Star

Caribbean Star
Karen Helsel
Amie Potter
106" x 106"

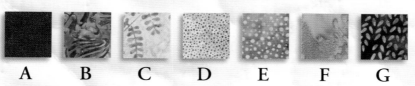

A B C D E F G

The key shows the position of each fabric in the quilt, and how strips are sewn together.

Making Section One for Seven Color Star

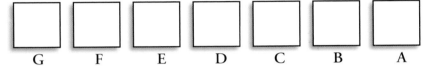

1. Pencil in color names of your fabrics, or paste in small fabric swatches.

G F E D C B A

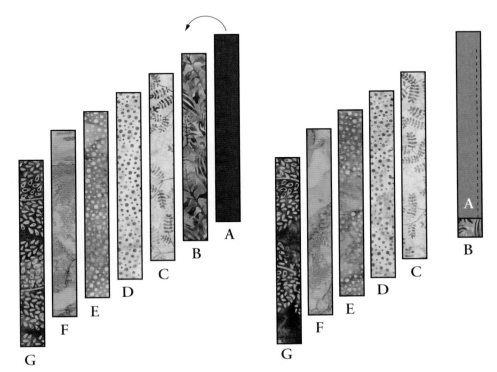

2. Line up one 2½" strip of each fabric in this order. Offset each strip 2". **Work from right to left.**

3. Flip Fabric A to Fabric B, right sides together, lengthwise.

4. Sew with A on top, wrong side up, and B underneath, 2" down from top of A. Open.

5. Sew on Fabric C, D, E, F, and G in same offset order.

6. **Complete a second set of Section One.**

7. Press seams to one side **away from Fabric A** and label as Section One. See page 33.

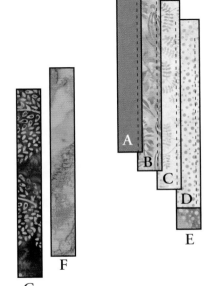

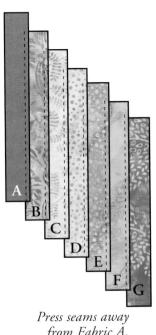

Press seams away from Fabric A.

Making Section Two for Seven Color Star

1. Pencil in color names of your fabrics, or paste in small fabric swatches.

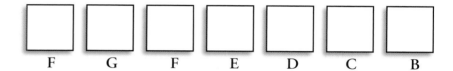

F G F E D C B

2. Line up one 2½" strip of each fabric in this order. **Offset each strip 2". Work from right to left.**

3. Flip Fabric B to Fabric C, right sides together, lengthwise.

4. Sew with B on top, wrong side up, and C underneath, 2" down from top of B. Open.

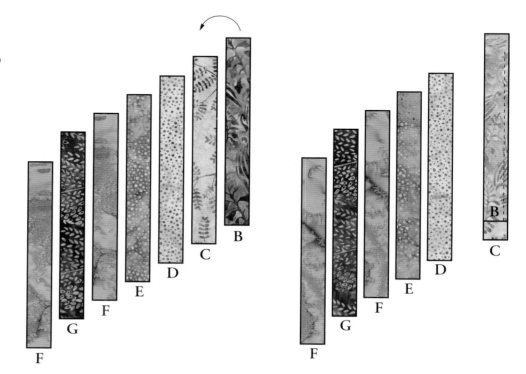

5. Sew on Fabrics D, E, F, G and F in same offset order.

6. **Complete a second set** of **Section Two**.

7. Carefully press seams to one side **away from Fabric B** and label as Section Two.

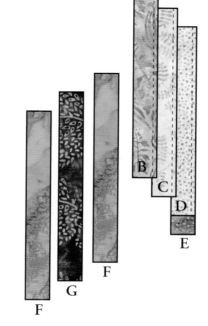

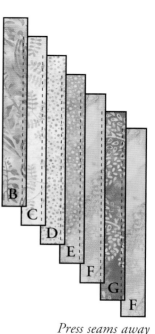

Press seams away from Fabric B.

Making Section Three for Seven Color Star

1. Pencil in color names of your fabrics, or paste in small fabric swatches.

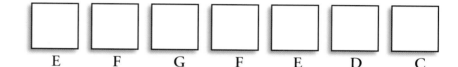

E   F   G   F   E   D   C

2. Line up one 2½" strip of each fabric in this order. **Offset each strip 2". Work from right to left.**

3. Flip Fabric C to Fabric D, right sides together, lengthwise.

4. Sew with C on top, wrong side up, and D underneath, 2" down from top of C. Open.

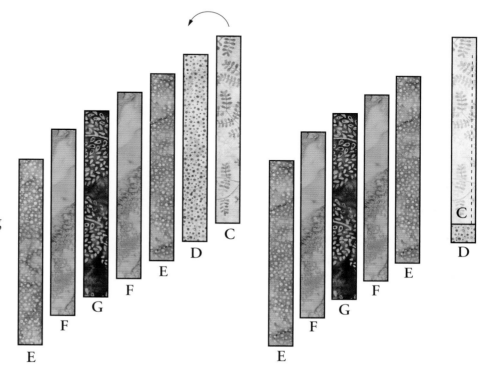

5. Sew on Fabric E, F, G, F, and E in same offset order.

6. **Complete a second set** of Section Three.

7. Press seams to one side **away from Fabric C** and label as Section Three.

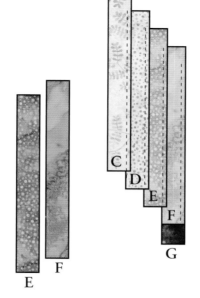

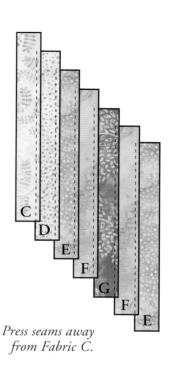

Press seams away from Fabric C.

Making Section Four for Seven Color Star

1. Pencil in color names of your fabrics, or paste in small fabric swatches.

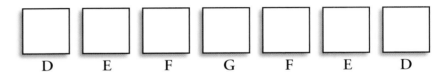

D E F G F E D

2. Line up one 2½" strip of each fabric in this order. **Offset each strip 2". Work from right to left.**

3. Flip Fabric D to Fabric E, right sides together, lengthwise.

4. Sew with D on top, wrong side up, and E underneath, 2" down from top of D. Open.

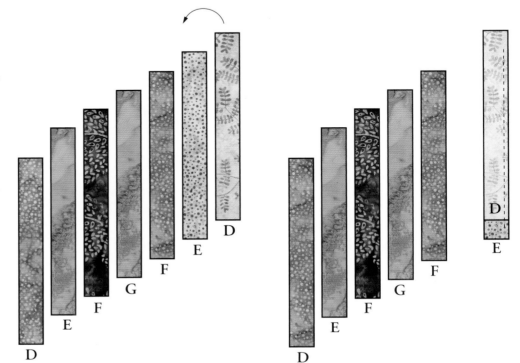

5. Sew on Fabric F, G, F, E and D in same offset order.

6. **Complete one set** of Section Four.

7. Press seams to one side **away from Fabric D** and label as Section Four.

8. Continue to **Cutting Diamond Strips** on page 43.

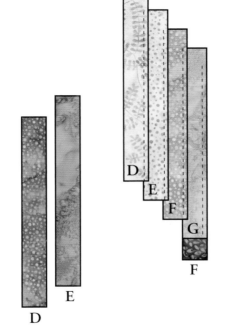

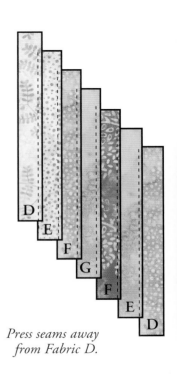

Press seams away from Fabric D.

Cutting Diamond Strips

Instructions are the same for Four, Six, and Seven Color Stars.

Selecting the right ruler for cutting Diamond strips carefully and accurately is important.

Select one of the **three different rulers** suggested for cutting Diamond strips. Directions for cutting right handed or left handed are included.

Cutting Diamonds with 6" x 24" Ruler

This ruler must have a 45° line on it. So it doesn't slip while cutting, put InvisiGrip on bottom side. For cutting instructions, see pages 44 and 45.

Cutting Diamonds with Bias Stripper

This ruler is the most accurate for cutting Diamond strips. It can also be used for cutting 2¼" bias strips for bias binding. See pages 46 and 47.

Cutting Diamonds with Set In Triangle Ruler

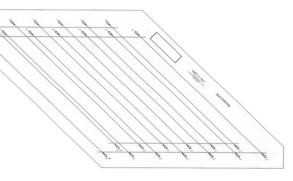

This ruler is versatile for cutting Diamond strips, squaring completed Diamonds, and cutting Side Triangles. See pages 48 and 49.

General Rules

1. Cut sixteen Diamond strips from each section. Cut only eight Diamond Strips from King Section Four.

2. Remaining strips can be cut in same manner for practice or used later in Borders. Save slightly imperfect ones for Border. You should get approximately eleven diamond strips per section.

3. You may need to correct your angle after several cuts. If any part of 2½" Diamond is wider, cut again to correct width.

Right Handed Cutting with 6" x 24" Ruler
Carefully handle cut Diamond strips.

1. Line up **Section One** on cutting mat with **Fabric A across top.**

2. Find **45° line** on ruler.

3. Place ruler's 45° line across bottom edge and line up with cutting mat. Follow photograph carefully.

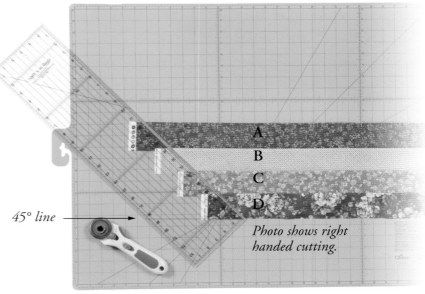

45° line →

Photo shows right handed cutting.

Strip set is right side up with A across top. Quilt in a Day Ruler is upside down to use 45° line.

4. Trim off left end on 45° angle with rotary cutter.

5. Pick up and move ruler to right until ruler's 2½" lines are on angled cut. Line up ruler's 45° line with bottom edge. Make sure that 45° line is parallel with horizontal lines on cutting mat. Cut.

6. Carefully and accurately **cut sixteen diamond strips 2½" wide from Section One. Do not press.**

7. **Continue to cut sixteen Diamond strips 2½" wide from each section with first fabric across top. Do not press.**

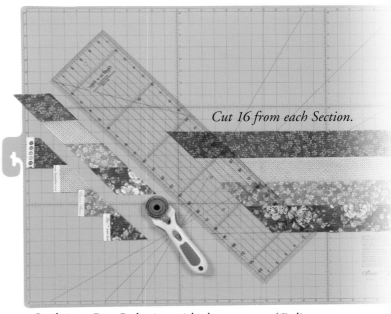

Cut 16 from each Section.

Quilt in a Day Ruler is upside down to use 45° line.

Left Handed Cutting with 6" x 24" Ruler

Carefully handle cut Diamond strips.

1. Turn strip set **wrong side up** with Fabric A across bottom.

2. Line up **Section One** on cutting mat with **Fabric A across bottom**.

3. Find **45° line** on ruler.

4. Place ruler's 45° line across bottom edge. Follow photograph carefully.

5. Trim off right end on 45° angle with rotary cutter.

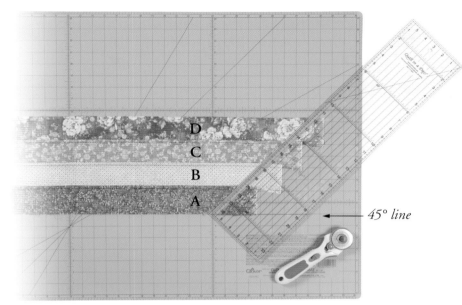

Strip set is wrong side up with A across bottom.

6. Pick up and move ruler to left until ruler's 2½" lines are on angled cut. Line up ruler's 45° line with bottom edge. Cut.

7. Carefully and accurately **cut sixteen diamond strips 2½" wide from Section One. Do not press.**

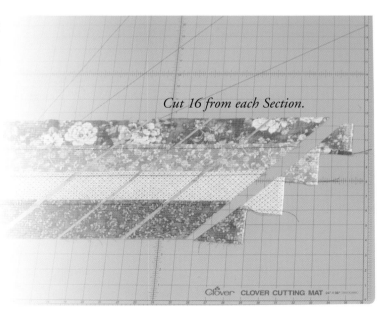

Cut 16 from each Section.

8. **Continue to cut sixteen Diamond strips 2½" wide from each section with first fabric across bottom, wrong side up. Do not press.**

Right Handed Cutting with Bias Stripper

Carefully handle cut Diamond strips.

1. Line up Section One on cutting mat with Fabric A across top. Line up strips with lines on cutting mat.

2. Place Bias Stripper on left end of strips.

3. Line up red line **with 2½" marks across bottom of strips.** Make sure first diagonal slit on cutter is in from selvage edge.

4. Put rotary cutter blade in first 2½" slot. Cut away from you, keeping cutter in slot.

5. Move rotary cutter to next 2½" slot. Continue cutting 2½" Diamond strips.

Line up red line with 2½" marks across bottom of strips.

Cut 2½" Diamond strips.

6. After cutting sixth Diamond strip, pull Bias Stripper away. Pick up Stripper and move it to right.

7. Line up first diagonal slot with cut edge.

8. Continue to carefully and accurately **cut sixteen diamond strips 2½" wide from Section One. Do not press.**

9. **Cut sixteen Diamond strips 2½" wide from each section with first fabric across top. Do not press.**

Cut sixteen Diamond strips 2½" wide from each section.

Left Handed Cutting with Bias Stripper

Carefully handle cut Diamond strips.

1. Turn strips over so they are **wrong side up**. Line up Section One on cutting mat with Fabric A across bottom.

2. Line up strips with lines on cutting mat.

3. Flip Bias Stripper over so numbers are wrong side up.

4. Place Bias Stripper on right end of strips.

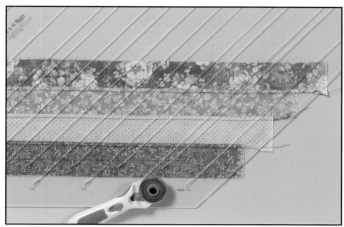

Flip Bias Stripper over so numbers are wrong side up.

5. Line up red line with **2½" marks across bottom of strips**. Make sure first diagonal slit on cutter is in from selvage edge.

6. Put rotary cutter blade in first 2½" slot. Cut away from you, keeping cutter in slot.

7. Continue cutting 2½" strips.

Line up red line with 2½" marks across bottom of strips.

8. After cutting sixth Diamond strip, pull Bias Stripper away. Pick up Stripper and move it to left.

9. Line up first diagonal slot with cut edge.

10. Continue to carefully and accurately **cut sixteen diamond strips 2½" wide from Section One. Do not press.**

11. **Cut sixteen Diamond strips 2½" wide from each section with first fabric across bottom, wrong side up. Do not press.**

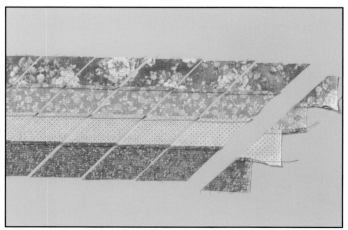

Cut sixteen Diamond strips 2½" wide from each section.

Right Handed Cutting with Set In Triangle Ruler

Carefully handle cut Diamond strips.

1. Line up Section One on cutting mat with Fabric A across top. Line up strips with lines on cutting mat.

2. Place Set In Triangle Ruler on left end of strips. One inch measurement is on bottom left.

3. Line up ruler's ¼" line with line on mat. Make sure edge of ruler is in from selvage edges.

4. Cut off selvages on diagonal.

Cut off selvages on diagonal.

5. Move ruler to right, lining up **2½" line with cut edge**, and cut 2½" Diamond strip.

Line up 2½" line with edge, and cut.

6. Continue to carefully and accurately **cut sixteen diamond strips 2½" wide from Section One. Do not press.**

7. **Cut sixteen Diamond strips 2½" wide from each section with first fabric across top. Do not press.**

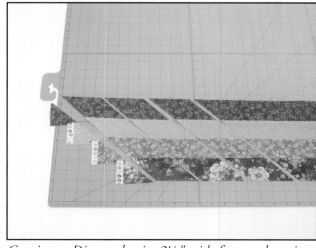

Cut sixteen Diamond strips 2½" wide from each section.

Left Handed Cutting with Set In Triangle Ruler

Carefully handle cut Diamond strips.

1. Turn strips over so they are wrong side up. Line up Section One on cutting mat with Fabric A across bottom. Line up strips with lines on cutting mat.

2. Place Set In Triangle Ruler on right end of strips. One inch measurement is on bottom right.

3. Line up ruler's ¼" line with line on mat. Make sure edge of ruler is in from selvage edges.

4. Cut off selvages on diagonal.

5. Move ruler to left, **lining up 2½" line with cut edge**, and cut 2½" Diamond strip.

6. Continue to carefully and accurately **cut sixteen Diamond strips 2½" wide from Section One. Do not press.**

7. **Cut sixteen Diamond strips 2½" wide from each section with first fabric across bottom, wrong side up. Do not press.**

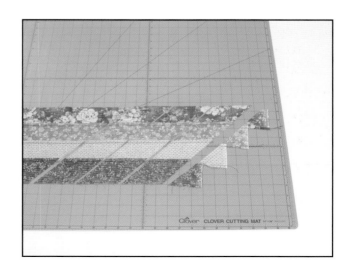

Arranging Diamonds

Arranging Diamonds for Four Color Star

1. Lay out stacks of Diamond strips with Section One on left and Section Two on right. Place sixteen Diamond strips in each stack.

2. Position top left tip of Section Two ⅜" higher than Section One.

3. Once sixteen sets are sewn, eight sets are turned and sewn into Diamonds.

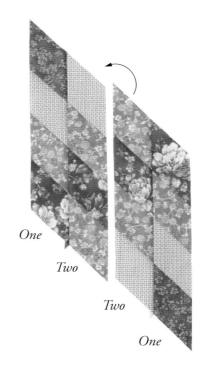

4. Eight complete Diamonds form the Star.

5. Turn to page 52 for sewing instructions.

Arranging Diamonds for Six Color Star

1. Lay out stacks of Diamond strips with Section One on left, Section Two in middle, and Section Three on right.

2. Position top left tip of Section Two and Three ⅜" higher.

3. Once sixteen sets are sewn, eight are turned and sewn into Diamonds.

4. Eight complete Diamonds form the Star.

5. Turn to next page for sewing instructions.

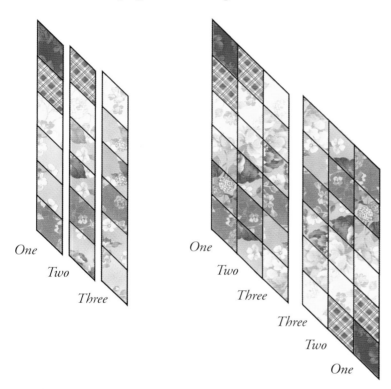

One
Two
Three

One
Two
Three
Three
Two
One

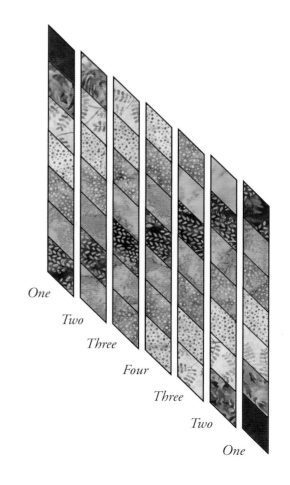

One
Two
Three
Four
Three
Two
One

Arranging Diamonds for Seven Color Star

1. *Because of the uneven number of sections, seven diamond strips are sewn together for one complete Diamond.* Lay out stacks of seven Diamond strips. Place eight Diamond strips in each stack.

2. Position top left tip of each section ⅜" higher.

3. When sewing Diamonds together, start at One and Two. Continue sewing one section at a time.

4. Eight complete Diamonds form the Star.

5. Turn to next page for sewing instructions.

Sewing Diamonds Together

1. Turn Section Two wrong side up.

2. With ruler and mechanical pencil, mark dots ¼" in from edge on seams of both Diamond strips. When drawing line, back your ruler off just enough to allow for pencil lead width.

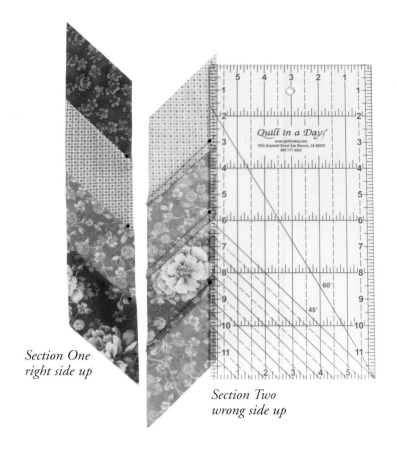

Section One right side up

Section Two wrong side up

3. Position Section One and Section Two **right sides together**, with tip of Section Two approximately ⅜" above Section One, and tip of Section One hanging out ⅜" at bottom.

4. Push pin through first match point on Section Two to match point on Section One underneath. For best results, pins should be very fine glass head pins.

5. Match all points with pins in this manner.

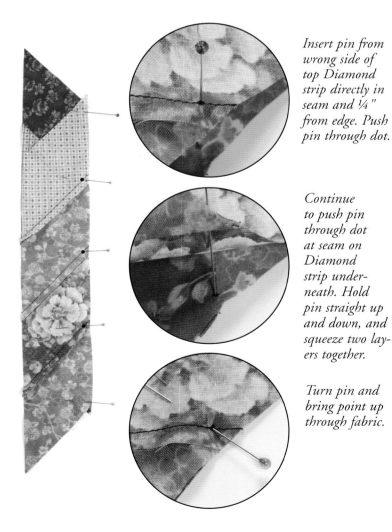

Insert pin from wrong side of top Diamond strip directly in seam and ¼" from edge. Push pin through dot.

Continue to push pin through dot at seam on Diamond strip underneath. Hold pin straight up and down, and squeeze two layers together.

Turn pin and bring point up through fabric.

6. Machine baste stitch this one set with 10 stitches per inch, pulling out each pin one stitch before sewing over match. Your needle and stitching line must cross match points exactly.

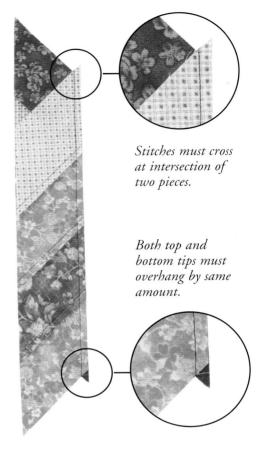

Stitches must cross at intersection of two pieces.

Both top and bottom tips must overhang by same amount.

7. Check your matches from right side.

8. If you are not satisfied with match, carefully remove your basting stitches, press, and try again until you have mastered the technique. Re-stitch with 15 stitches to the inch.

9. Once matching is mastered, you may be able to finger match and hold seams together with stiletto to eliminate pinning.

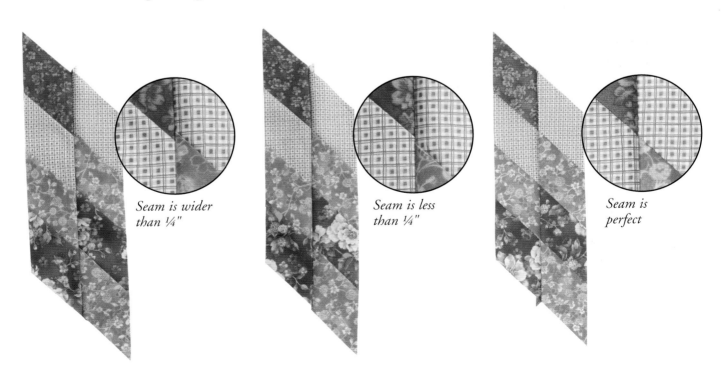

Seam is wider than ¼"

Seam is less than ¼"

Seam is perfect

The less you rip out seams, the less distorted the Diamonds will become. Handle Diamond strips gently.

Sewing Diamonds Together

1. Set stitch length to 15 stitches per inch.

2. Carefully match and pin each Diamond strip together.

3. Sew first set, pulling out each pin one stitch before sewing over match point.

4. **Four Color Stars:** Assembly-line sew Section One and Two.

5. **Six Color Stars:** Assembly-line sew Section One, Two and Three.

6. **Seven Color Stars:** Sew seven sections together into eight Diamonds.

Sewing Sets Together into Diamonds

1. **Four and Six Color Stars:** Sew sixteen sets together.

2. Sort sets into two equal stacks of eight each.

3. Turn right stack.

4. Assembly-line sew together to form eight large diamonds. Match and pin as you sew.

5. Gently press seams to one side.

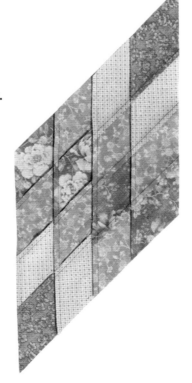

Measuring Sides of Diamonds

Each Diamond has a stretchy side, and a more stable side. So that Stars lie flat around outside edges after Side Triangles and Corners are sewn in, it is important to recognize these sides. You can see the difference in the grain of fabric.

Stretchy Side

The side with the greatest stretch is the side that is made of a Diamond strip cut on the 45° angle. The fabric threads are at an angle to the edge. Because of a tendency to stretch, this side is sewn with Diamonds on the bottom next to the feed dogs. Feed dogs help to ease in the stretch.

Stable Side

The more stable side is the one made up of one Diamond from each strip. The fabric **threads are parallel with the edge**, and are on the straight of grain. Because of its stability, this side is sewn with Diamonds on top.

1. Measure Diamonds with 6" x 24" Ruler, one side at a time.

2. Record your measurements from all sides.

3. Find average measurement and record.

4. Set aside Diamonds that need **sliver trimmed** on the sides or are larger than the average.

_____

Average Side Measurement

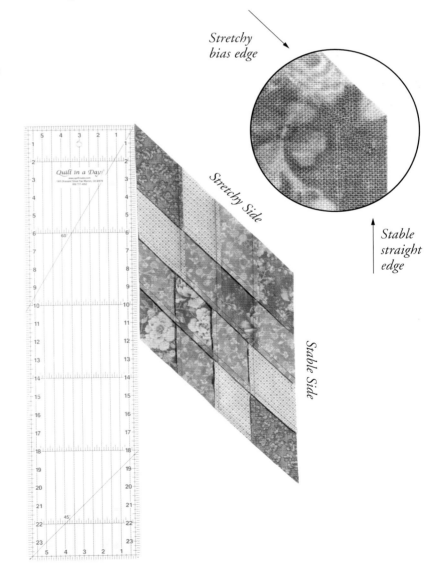

Stretchy bias edge

Stable straight edge

All diamonds should be approximately the same size.

**Checking and Trimming 45° Angle
of Each Diamond**

1. With right side up, place Diamond on cutting mat with point of Diamond fitting into 45° angle on mat.

2. **If Diamond is slightly more than 45°, sliver trim** outside edges with ruler and rotary cutter. Turn Diamond around and sliver trim again.

   Sliver trimming is ⅛" or less.

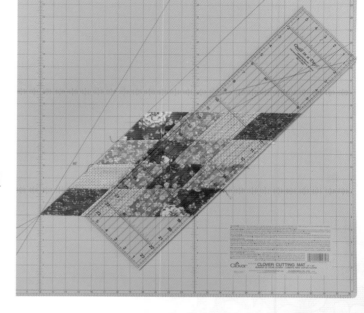

3. **If Diamond is slightly less than 45°, correct by placing on pressing mat and gently pressing across middle of Diamond with iron.** Check it against 45° angle on pressing mat and cutting mat.

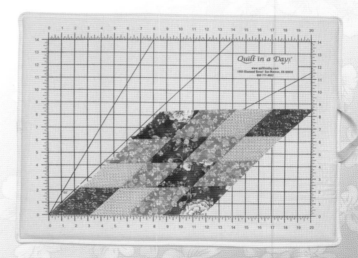

4. **Optional:** Check angle with Set In Triangle Ruler. Lay ruler on top of each Diamond with point of ruler fitting into point on Diamond, and straight edge of ruler lining up with sides of Diamond. Lines on ruler should be parallel with seams. **Sliver trim** if uneven.

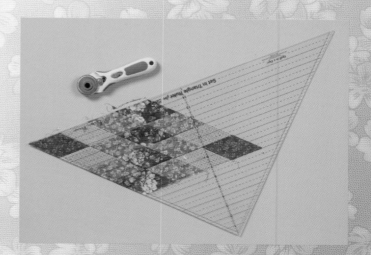

Sewing Stars Together

1. With right side up, lay out two stacks of Diamonds with four in each stack.

2. Place with center **seams going down on right** Diamonds, and seams **going up on left** Diamonds.

3. Flip Diamond on right onto Diamond on left. Make sure seams lie in opposite directions. Lock seams.

4. Draw short lines ¼" in from edges with 6" Square Up Ruler. Mark a dot at intersection.

5. Match and pin at top, each point on side, and ¼" in from bottom edge.

6. Stitch. End your stitching ¼" from outside edge. Lock stitches.

7. Stitch remaining Diamonds into quarters.

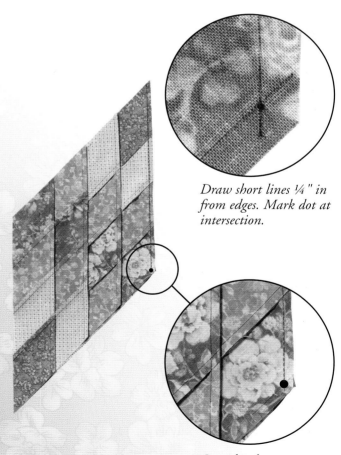

Draw short lines ¼" in from edges. Mark dot at intersection.

Outside edges must match. Trim to match if necessary.

8. From wrong side, gently press this seam to left.

9. Check 90° angle by placing 12½" Square Up Ruler's diagonal line on diagonal seam. **Sliver trim** if uneven.

10. Trim off tip from seam allowance.

Trim tip.

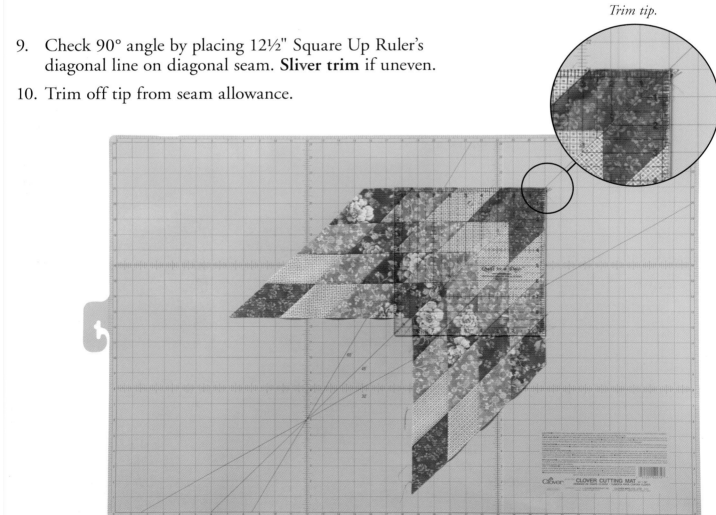

Sewing Quarters Together

1. Sew two Star quarters into halves from center out, **ending your stitching ¼" from outside edges.**

2. Press center seams to the left. Sliver trim if edges are not straight lines, **maintaining ¼" seam.**

End ¼" from outside edges.

3. Place two halves right sides together.

4. Carefully match and pin center point, pushing seams on top up and underneath seams down.

5. Sew across center with 2" of stitching. Check. Your seam allowance must match seam allowances on photograph.

6. Check on right side. If it does not match, remove stitches and make adjustments.

7. Continue to sew two halves together from center outward. **Do not stitch last ¼" on outside edges.**

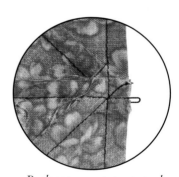

Push seam on top up and underneath seam down.

Swirling Center

1. Remove horizontal straight stitches in vertical seam allowance on both sides.

2. Lay Star flat wrong side up.

3. Open center and press flat, swirling seams around center.

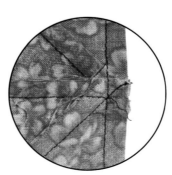

Remove straight stitches in vertical seam.

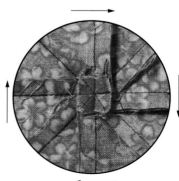

Swirl seams around center.

Corner Squares and Side Triangles

Sizes of Corners and Side Triangles are calculated from average length of side of Diamond. Refer to **your average side measurement** on page 55. Locate your Cutting Chart for Four, Six, or Seven Color Radiant Stars, and match your average Diamond side with calculations.

1. Background must be cut on grain. Trim and remove selvages before cutting pieces. Pay particular attention to layout for correct use of yardage.

2. If not cut already, cut length strips for your quilt. Refer to your yardage chart on pages 10 – 21.

3. Cut four solid squares for Corners. **Do not cut squares if you plan to make optional Stars for Corners (page 80) or substitute a Stripe for part of Background (page 66).**

4. Two methods are given for cutting Side Triangles. Cut one large square or strips half the width of large square. You need the Set In Triangle Ruler for cutting strips.

Four Color Star

Average Diamond Side			Four Corner Squares	Side Triangle Square	or	Two Strips for Triangles
10½"	+ ¼"	=	10¾"	15¼"		7⅝"
10¾"	+ ¼"	=	11"	15¾"		7⅞"
11"	+ ¼"	=	11¼"	16"		8"
11¼"	+ ¼"	=	11½"	16½"		8¼"
11½"	+ ¼"	=	11¾"	16¾"		8⅜"
11¾"	+ ¼"	=	12"	17"		8½"

Use this chart for Four Color Wallhanging, Lap and Twin.

A 20" Square Up Ruler is best for cutting Four Color Corner Squares. For Side Triangles, cut one large square or two strips.

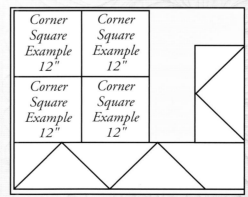

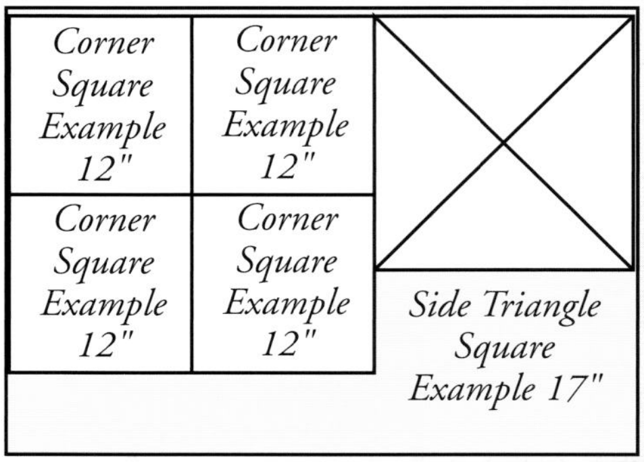

Corner Square Example 12" Corner Square Example 12"
Corner Square Example 12" Corner Square Example 12"
Side Triangle Square Example 17"

or

Corner Square Example 12" Corner Square Example 12"
Corner Square Example 12" Corner Square Example 12"

Strips for Triangles Example 8½"

Six Color Star

Average Diamond Side			Four Corner Squares	Side Triangle Square	or	Two Strips
16"	+ ¼"	=	16¼"	23"		11½"
16¼"	+ ¼"	=	16½"	23½"		11¾"
16½"	+ ¼"	=	16¾"	23¾"		11⅞"
16¾"	+ ¼"	=	17"	24¼"		12⅛"
17"	+ ¼"	=	17¼"	24½"		12¼"
17¼"	+ ¼"	=	17½"	24¾"		12⅜"

Use this chart for Six Color Wallhanging and Queen.

A 20" Square Up Ruler is best for cutting Four Color Corner Squares. For Side Triangle Square, use measurements on large cutting mat with 6"x 24" ruler, or cut two strips.

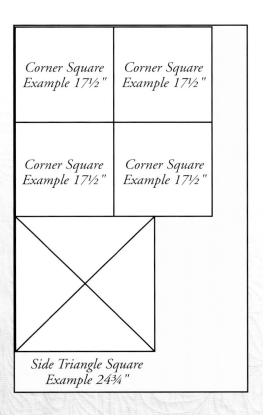

or

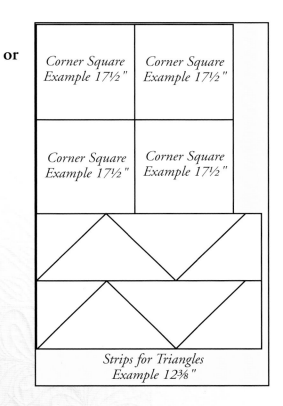

Seven Color Star

Average Diamond Side			Four Corner Squares	Side Triangle Square	or	One Strip
19¼"	+ ¼" =		19½"	27¾"		13⅞"
19½"	+ ¼" =		19¾"	28"		14"
19¾"	+ ¼" =		20"	28½"		14¼"
20"	+ ¼" =		20¼"	28¾"		14⅜"
20¼"	+ ¼" =		20½"	29"		14½"
20½"	+ ¼" =		20¾"	29½"		14¾"

Use this chart for Seven Color King.

A 22" Square Up Ruler is best for cutting Seven Color Corner Squares. For Side Triangle Square, use measurements on large cutting mat with 6"x 24" ruler, and cut one large square or one strip.

Based on 42" wide fabric

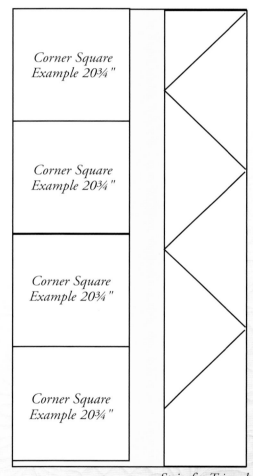

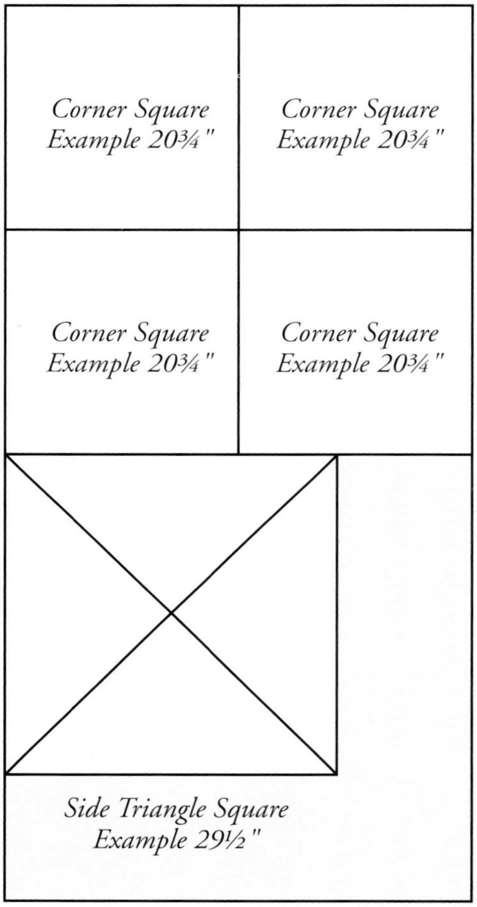

Corner Square Example 20¾"

Corner Square Example 20¾"

Corner Square Example 20¾"

Corner Square Example 20¾"

Side Triangle Square Example 29½"

or

Corner Square Example 20¾"

Corner Square Example 20¾"

Corner Square Example 20¾"

Corner Square Example 20¾"

Strip for Triangles Example 14¾"

Cutting Large Square into Four Side Triangles

1. Cut one square on diagonals twice to make four triangles.

2. Use an extra long plexiglas ruler and rotary cutter, or mark lines with yardstick and then cut.

Or Cutting Triangles from Strips (Optional)

Use Set In Triangle Ruler from Quilt in a Day.

1. Cut Background strip of fabric to calculated width.

2. Place tip of Set In Triangle at top of strip. Line up bottom edge of strip with line on Triangle.

3. Cut triangle.

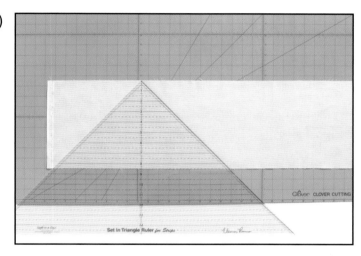

4. Turn Triangle with tip pointing down. Cut second triangle.

5. Continue cutting four triangles.

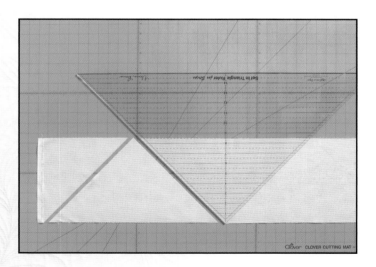

Sewing in Side Triangles

The stretchy diamond side, or left side, is sewn first, with Diamonds on bottom.

1. **On wrong side**, draw short lines ¼" in from edges. Mark dot at intersection.

2. Place triangles around Star. Flip triangle to left, right sides together to Diamond.

3. Push a pin through penciled dot on triangle to point where seam ended ¼" from outside edge on Star. Match tips on outside edges and pin. *Triangle side may be ¼" longer than Diamond side.*

4. Sew from ¼" point outward, with Diamonds on bottom.

5. Flip Star so that Diamonds are now on top with wrong side up. Match ¼" point. Pin outside edges. **Do not stretch either piece excessively. Excess Background fabric can be trimmed later.**

6. Sew all Sides Triangles in this manner. Press seams toward triangles.

Sewing Square in Each Corner

1. Pencil a dot in corner on **wrong side** of each square ¼" from outside edges.

2. Flip square to left, right sides together to Diamond. Push pin through penciled dot on square and ¼" point where seam ended. Match square to outside edges on Diamond. Sew from ¼" point outward with Diamonds on bottom. **Do not stretch any piece excessively.**

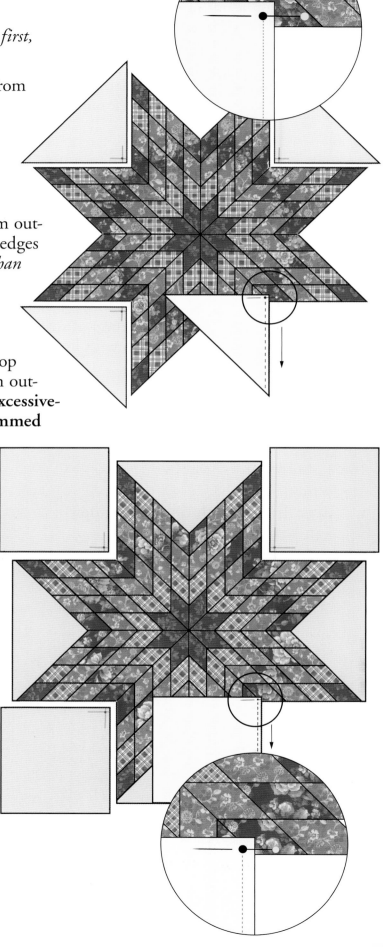

3. Flip Star in half so Diamonds are now on top with wrong side up. Match and sew in second side.

4. Sew all Corner Squares in this manner.

5. Press seams toward Corner Squares.

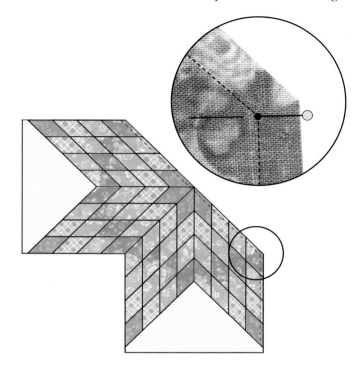

Trimming Outside Edges

It may be necessary to straighten outside edges. Be careful not to trim off Star points and ¼" seam allowances, or distort square shape of Star.

1. Lay Star on large gridded mat, and check if sides need to be squared.

2. Place ¼" line on 6" x 24" ruler on tips of Star points. Sliver trim to straighten without removing ¼" seam allowance.

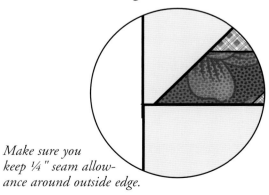

Make sure you keep ¼" seam allowance around outside edge.

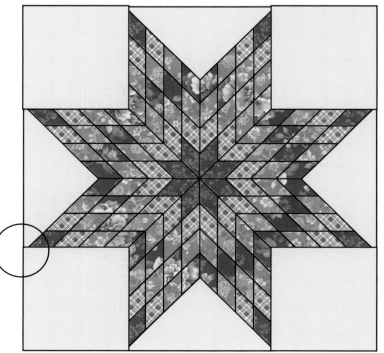

Optional Striped Corners and Triangles

Four Color Star
Select 1 yard fabric with stripes approximately 4½" wide across width of fabric.

Six Color Star
Select 2 yards fabric with stripes approximately 7½" wide across width of fabric.

Seven Color Star
Select 2½ yards fabric with stripes approximately 9½" wide across width of fabric.

Six color example quilt on back cover used a 7½" wide Border stripe.

1. **Side Triangles:** Measure width of your stripe.

2. Multiply width of stripe by 2.

3. Cut stripes the complete length of fabric.

Example: Six Color Star

7½" Width of Strips
x 2
_____
15"

4. Find size of Side Triangle Square based on average side of Diamond. See charts on pages 60-62. Example is 24½".

5. Subtract width of stripe doubled from size of Side Triangle Square. Add 1" for seam allowances.

Example: Six Color Star

24½" Side Triangle Square
- 15" Width of Stripe Doubled
_____
9½"
+ 1" for Seam Allowances
_____
10½" Size of Side Triangle Square

6. Cut one Side Triangle Square. Cut on both diagonals into four triangles.

7. Cut four Border strips 2½" longer than original size of Side Triangle Square.

8. Find center of triangle and center of stripe. Pin, sew together and press seam to triangle.

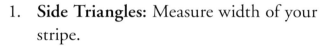

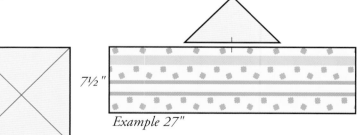

7½"

Example 27"

Example 10½" square

9. With 6" x 24" ruler, trim stripe with sides of triangle. Optional: Use Set In Triangle Ruler.

10. Inset triangle into Star. See page 64.

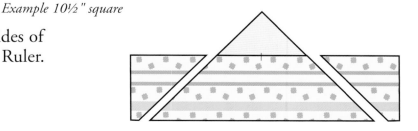

1. **Corners:** Begin with size for your Corner Squares. See pages 61-63.

2. Subtract width of stripe from size of Corner Square.

3. Add ½" for seam allowance.

4. Cut four Corner squares this size.

Example: Six Color Star

17"	Size of Corner Squares
-7½"	Width of stripe
9½"	
+ ½"	Seams
10"	Size of Four Corner Squares

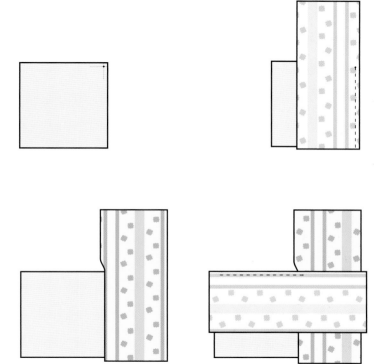

5. On right side of Four Corner Squares, mark a dot ¼" from one corner.

6. Cut stripe the length of **average Diamond** side plus 2½" for miter. Refer to page 55.

7. Pin and sew Border stripe from dot to edge of square.

8. Press open.

9. Repeat on second side, ending on dot.

10. **Miter:** Fold block diagonally right sides together and line up two stripes. Match lines on stripe with pins.

11. Line up diagonal line on 12½" Square Up Ruler with outside edge of stripes. Line up right edge of ruler with dot where stitches meet.

12. Draw a sewing line from outside edge to dot. Sew on drawn line. Trim, and press seams open.

13. Insert squares into corners. See page 64.

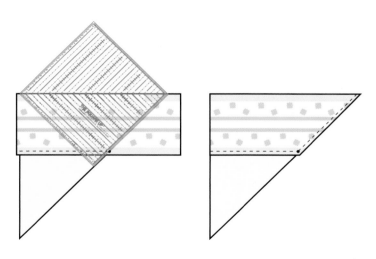

Adding Borders to Your Radiant Star

Be creative when adding Borders and Diamond strips. Suggested Border yardage, strip measurements, and Border examples have been given for each of the quilts. However, you may wish to custom design your Borders by changing widths of strips, adding Diamond strips to two sides, four sides, or not adding Diamond strips at all.

When custom fitting your quilt, lay the Star on the bed and measure to find how much Border is needed to get the fit you want. Keep in mind that the quilt will "shrink" approximately 3" in length and width with quilting.

Summer Radiance
Gail Yakos
Amie Potter

Gail's Star is festooned with six different borders. A pink first border creating the bold frame was only the beginning. Next, a diamond border separated by the white narrow one offers even more room for interesting quilting. Gail then added wider strips to elongate her creation and finished off with a happy large scale floral print.

Piecing Border and Binding Strips

1. Sew strips of each fabric into long pieces by assembly-line sewing.

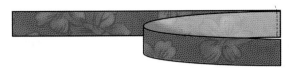

2. Take strip on top and fold it so right side is up.

3. Place third strip on top right sides together.

Lay first strip right side up. Lay second strip right sides to it. Backstitch, stitch short ends together, and backstitch again.

4. Continue assembly-line sewing all short ends together into long pieces for each fabric.

5. Clip threads holding strips together.

6. Press seams open.

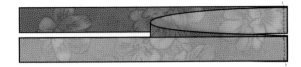

Adding Length Strips

When making lap, twin, and queen size Radiant Star quilts, Background length strips are added to two ends. You may want to add a Diamond strip between the Star and length strip.

For king size Radiant Star quilts, you may want to add a Diamond strip to four sides before adding Background strips.

Piecing and Adding Diamond Strip Border (Optional)

1. Assembly-line sew leftover Diamond strips together in random order into one long strip.

2. If Diamond strip is not long enough, make more Diamond strips by piecing extra strips from Star and cutting them on 45° angle.

3. Carefully measure sides, cut and pin in place.

4. Sew with Diamonds on bottom so bias does not stretch. Diamonds do not match at corners. If desired, place 2½" Cornerstones at corners.

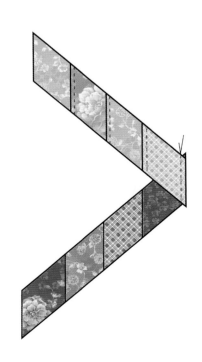

Sewing Borders to Radiant Star

*Once you decide on order of adding Diamond strips, lengths, or Borders,
follow these instructions.*

1. **Measure** outside edges of top. Measure through middle of top. Record each number and find average measurement for each side.

2. **Cut** two side strips that measurement.

3. **Pin** and sew to two opposite sides. Set seams with Borders on top. Open, and press seams toward Borders.

4. For top and bottom, measure through middle and ends from outside edge to outside edge. Find average measurement.

5. Cut two strips that measurement.

6. **Pin** and sew to top and bottom. Set seams with Borders on top. Open, and press seams toward Border.

7. All Borders are added in this manner.

Quilting Your Radiant Star

Long Arm Quilting

Some quilters prefer to complete a top and send it to a long arm quilter. Follow these instructions if long arm quilting is your choice.

1. Clip loose threads. Make sure there are no loose or unsewn seams. Have top free of embellishments.

2. Press top and backing. Have them as wrinkle free as possible.

3. Measure top. Side measurements and top and bottom measurements should be the same.

4. Backing should be 8" longer and wider than quilt top. If quilt top is 90" x 108", then backing should be 98" x 116".

5. Batting should be no less than 8" longer and wider than the pieced top measurements.

6. **Do not pin the three layers together.**

Eleanor's stunning Wallhanging is made from 2½" Jelly Roll strips. She divided one Jelly Roll into four color families that blended well. Following yardage chart on page 11, she placed colors according to the number of strips needed and what she had available.

Amie Potter, the long arm quilter, stitched in the ditch around the Star and Diamond border. She quilted feathered hearts with crosshatching in the background, finishing with a very fancy echoed feather in the outside border. Beautiful!

Quilting on a Conventional Machine

If you wish to free motion quilt Background squares and Triangles, mark lines before layering backing and batting.

Marking Corner Squares

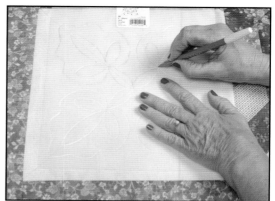

1. Select an appropriate continuous line stencil slightly smaller then size of Corner Squares.

2. To help center stencil, draw X on square with disappearing pen and 6" x 24" Ruler.

3. Center stencil on square and draw lines through slots.

4. Remove stencil and check that all lines are drawn. Connect broken lines if desired.

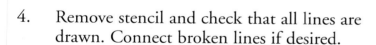

Marking Side Triangles

1. To help center stencil, draw straight line from inside point to opposite side.

2. Divide same continuous line stencil into fourths on diagonals.

3. Place stencil on triangle and draw lines through slots.

Layering Your Quilt

The trend today is to make the backing as creative and exciting as the front of the quilt. As an option, add a dash of color down the center backing seam with left-over diamond strips. Sew left-over strips in random order across the top of the backing, only to be daringly revealed when the quilt is turned back for the night.

1. If necessary, piece Backing approximately 8" larger than finished top.

2. Spread out Backing on a large table or floor area, **right side down**. Clamp fabric to edge of table with quilt clips, or tape Backing to the floor. Do not stretch Backing.

3. Layer Batting on Backing, also 8" larger than finished top. Pat flat.

4. With right side up, center quilt on Batting and Backing. Smooth until all layers are flat. Clamp or tape outside edges.

Safety Pinning

1. Place pin covers on 1" safety pins with pliers.

2. Pin away from where you plan to quilt. Catch tip of pin in grooves on pinning tool, and close pins.

3. Safety pin through all layers three to five inches apart.

4. Use pinning tool to open pins when removing them. Store pins opened.

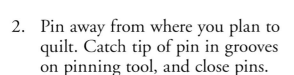

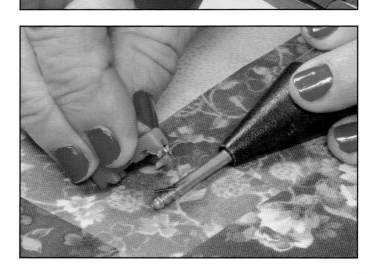

"Stitch in the Ditch" on Diamond and Border Seams

1. Place walking foot on sewing machine. Change stitch length to 3.0 or 10 stitches per inch. Use center needle position. Use a thread that blends with your Star on top, and a thread matching your backing in the bobbin.

Walking Foot

2. Roll corner of quilt to Star. Hold "roll" in place with quilt clamps. Place hands on quilt in triangular shape, and spread seams open. Stitch in the ditch, anchoring Diamonds.

3. For large sizes, "free motion" stitch around Stars so you don't have to continuously turn quilt.

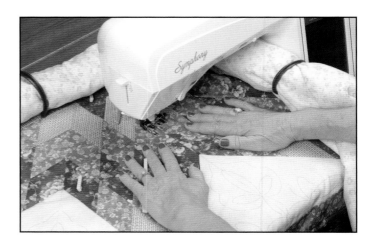

4. Stitch in the ditch along Border seams.

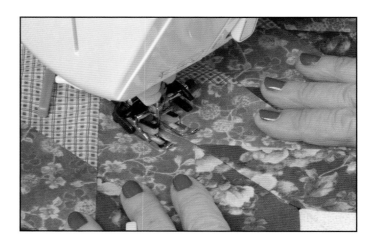

Quilting Corners with Straight Stitches

1. Line up diagonal line on Square Up Ruler with diagonal line on Star.

2. Slide Square Up Ruler onto Background square, matching square lines on ruler with corner seams. Mark square lines evenly spaced.

3. With 6" x 24" ruler, extend lines across Side Triangles.

4. Quilt on the lines.

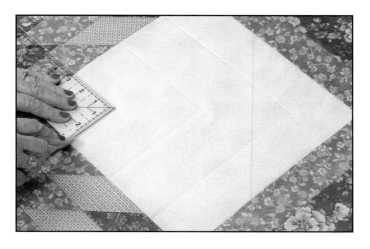

Quilting with Darning Foot

1. Attach darning foot to sewing machine. Drop feed dogs or cover feed dogs with a plate. No stitch length is required as you control the length by your sewing speed. Use a fine needle and regular thread in the top and regular thread to match the Backing in the bobbin. Use needle down position.

2. Optional: Wear quilter's gloves to help grip quilt.

3. Place hands flat around marked design. Bring bobbin thread up on line.

4. Lock stitch and clip thread tails. Free motion stitch **on marked lines**. Keep top of block at top. Sew sideways and back and forth without turning quilt.

5. Lock stitches and cut threads.

Use matching thread. Black thread was used for illustration purposes.

Adding Binding

1. Square off selvage edges on 3" Binding strips. Assembly-line sew short ends to make one continuous strip.

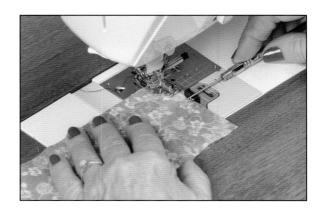

2. Press seams open.

3. Fold and press in half lengthwise with **wrong sides together**.

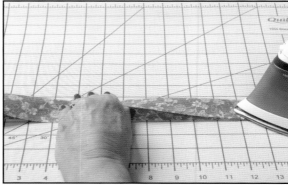

Press in half lengthwise with wrong sides together.

4. Place walking foot attachment on sewing machine, and regular thread on top and in bobbin to match Binding.

5. In middle of one side, line up raw edges of folded Binding with raw edges of quilt. Begin stitching 4" from end of Binding. Sew with 10 stitches per inch, or 3.0 to 3.5. Sew approximately ⅜" from edge, or width of walking foot.

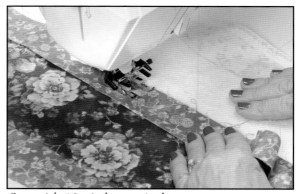

Sew with 10 stitches per inch.

6. Place pin ⅜" from corner of quilt.

7. At corner, stop stitching at pin ⅜" in from edge with needle in fabric. Raise presser foot and turn quilt toward corner.

8. Put presser foot down. Stitch diagonally off edge of Binding.

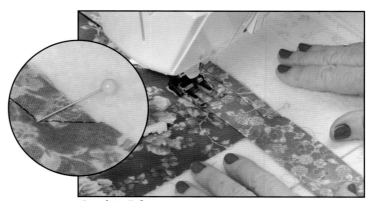

Stitch ⅜" from corner.

9. Raise foot, and pull quilt forward slightly.

10. Turn quilt to next side. Remove pin.

11. Fold Binding strip straight up on diagonal. Fingerpress diagonal fold.

Fold Binding strip straight up on diagonal.

12. Fold Binding strip straight down with diagonal fold underneath. Line up top of fold with raw edge of Binding underneath.

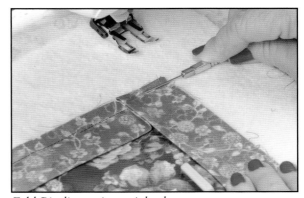
Fold Binding strip straight down.

13. Begin sewing from edge.

14. Continue stitching and mitering corners around outside of quilt.

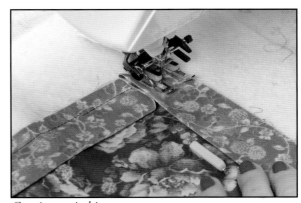
Continue stitching.

15. Stop stitching 4" from where ends will overlap.

16. Line up two ends of Binding. Trim excess with ½" overlap.

Trim excess with ½" overlap.

17. Pull ends away from quilt. Line up newly cut edges.

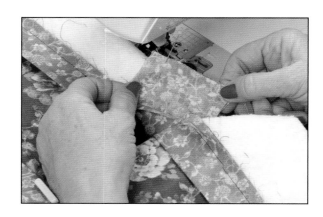

18. Sew a ¼" seam.

19. Press seam open.

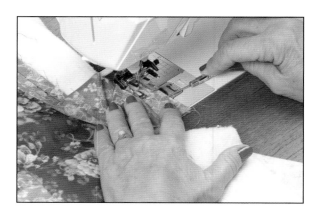

20. Continue stitching Binding in place.

21. Trim Batting and Backing up to ⅛" from raw edges of Binding.

22. Fold back Binding.

23. Pull Binding to back side of quilt.

24. Pin in place so that folded edge on Binding covers stitching line. Tuck in excess fabric at each miter on diagonal.

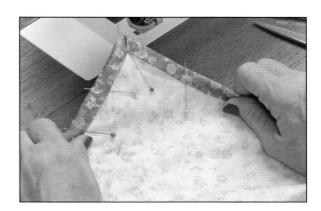

25. From right side, "stitch in the ditch" using invisible or matching thread on front side, and bobbin thread to match Binding on back side. Catch folded edge of Binding on the back side with stitching.

   Optional: Hand stitch Binding in place.

26. Hand stitch miters.

27. Sew identification label on Back.

   • name of maker
   • place where quilt was made
   • year
   • name of quilt
   • any other pertinent information.

Making Optional Stars for Corners

Make little Stars and sew into corners in place of one piece Corner Squares.

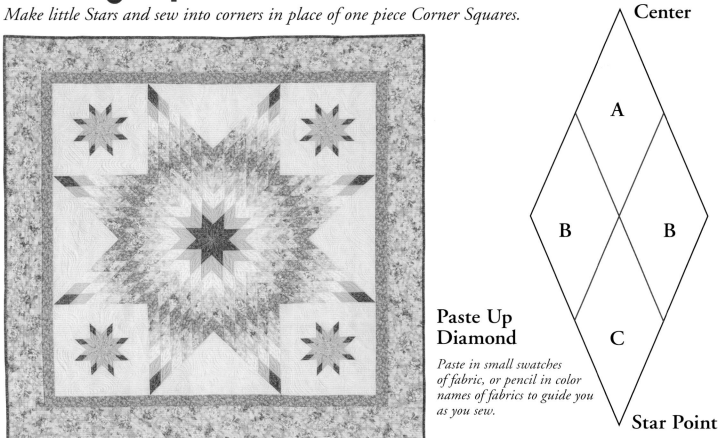

Center

A

B   B

C

Star Point

Paste Up Diamond

Paste in small swatches of fabric, or pencil in color names of fabrics to guide you as you sew.

Yardage for Corners Only

		Four Color Star 10" Little Stars	Six Color Star 10" Little Stars	Seven Color Star 15" Little Stars
	Fabric A Center	⅛ yd (2) 1½" strips	⅛ yd (2) 1½" strips	¼ yd (4) 2" strips
	Fabric B Radiant	¼ yd (4) 1½" strips	¼ yd (4) 1½" strips	⅝ yd (8) 2" strips
	Fabric C Star Points	⅛ yd (2) 1½" strips	⅛ yd (2) 1½" strips	¼ yd (4) 2" strips
	Background Blocks *Use Background purchased following yardage charts on pages 10-21.* Framing	(2) 4¼" strips cut into (16) 4¼" squares (2) 3½" strips cut into (16) 3½" squares (6) 1½" strips	(2) 4¼" strips cut into (16) 4¼" squares (2) 3½" strips cut into (16) 3½" squares (2) 10½" strips cut into (8) 10½" squares	(2) 5½" strips cut into (16) 5½" squares (2) 4½" strips cut into (16) 4½" squares (8) 3½" strips

First number in black is for Four and Six Color Radiant Stars. Little Stars are 10" square.
Second number in red ( ) is for Seven Color Radiant Star. Little Stars are 15" square.

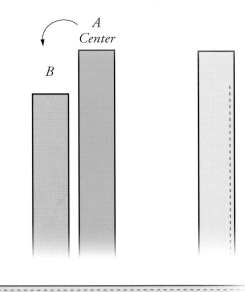

Making Section One

1. Place one 1½" (2") strip each of A and B. Offset strips by 1½" (2"). Flip A to B, right sides together.

2. Sew with Fabric A on top.

3. Set seam with B on top.

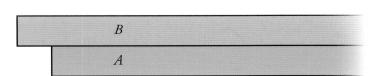

4. Open, and press seam toward B.
5. Make second set of strips

Making Section Two

1. Place one 1½" (2") strip each of B and C. Offset strips by 1½" (2"). Flip B to C, right sides together.

2. Sew with Fabric B on top.

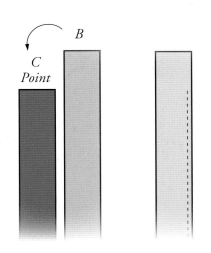

3. Set seam with C on top.

Set seam with C on top.

4. Open, and press seam toward C.
5. Make second set of strips.

Cutting Diamonds with 6" Square Up Ruler

Illustration shows 1½" line

1. Turn 6" Square Up Ruler to under side.

2. Put Glow Line Tape on 1½" (2") line.

3. Line up Section One on cutting mat with Fabric A across top.

4. Find 45° line on 6" Square Up Ruler. Line up 45° line across bottom edge on left. Illustration shows Quilt in a Day's 6" Square Up Ruler. Your ruler may be different.

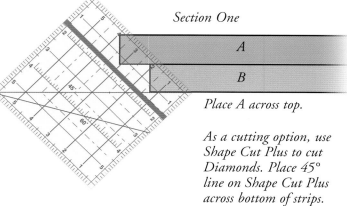

Section One

A

B

Place A across top.

As a cutting option, use Shape Cut Plus to cut Diamonds. Place 45° line on Shape Cut Plus across bottom of strips.

5. Trim off left end on 45° angle.

6. Slide Ruler to right, keeping 45° angle across bottom of strip. Line up Ruler's 1½" (2") line on cut edge. Cut again.

7. Continue to cut a total of thirty-two Diamonds.

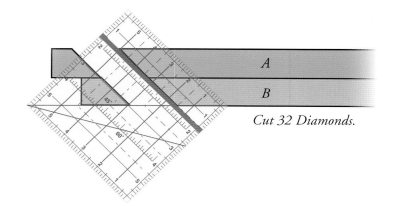

A

B

Cut 32 Diamonds.

8. Repeat cutting Section Two with Fabric B across top.

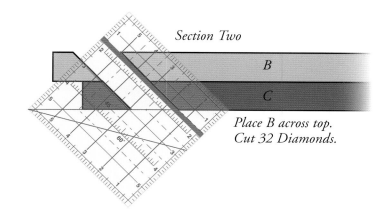

Section Two

B

C

Place B across top.
Cut 32 Diamonds.

Sewing Diamond Strips Together

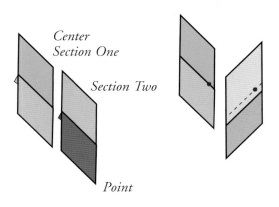

1. Lay out one set of Diamond strips with Section One on left, and Section Two on right. Position tip of Section Two slightly higher than Section One.

2. Turn Section Two wrong side up. Mark match points ¼" in on both strips with mechanical pencil.

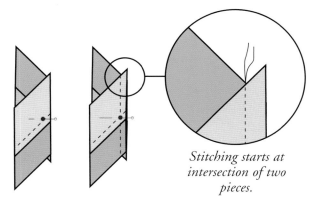

3. Push a pin through match point ¼" in on Section Two to ¼" match point on Section One.

4. Sew one set, pulling out pin one stitch before you sew over match. Your needle and stitching line must cross match point exactly.

Stitching starts at intersection of two pieces.

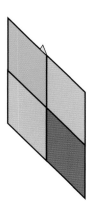

5. Check your match from the right side. Make adjustments if necessary.

6. Continue assembly-line sewing a total of thirty-two sets of Diamonds for four Stars.

Pressing Diamonds

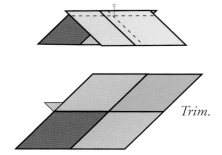

1. Place Diamond on pressing mat with Section One on top, wrong side up. Set seam.

2. Open and press toward Section One.

3. Place ruler's 45° angle on Diamond. Trim tip even with Diamond.

Trim.

Sewing Four Quarters

1. Lay out pair of Diamonds. Stack four sets for each Star.

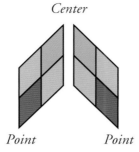

Center

Point   *Point*

2. Cut four Large 4¼" (5½") Squares in half on one diagonal for each Star.

3. Place with Diamonds right sides up.

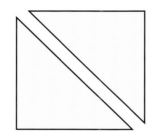

4. Cut four Small 3½" (4½") Squares in half on one diagonal for each Star.

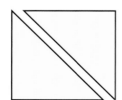

5. Place with Diamonds right sides up.

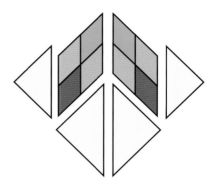

6. Divide into Left Half and Right Half.

 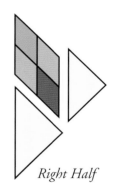

Left Half   *Right Half*

 **Sewing Right Half**

1. Lay out Right Half.

2. Flip Diamond right sides together to Large Triangle on left.

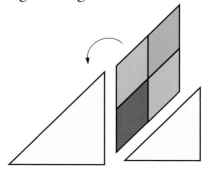

3. Let ⅜" tip hang over on top edge. Assembly-line sew.

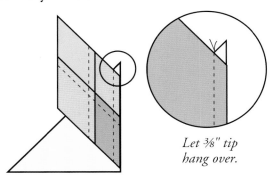

Let ⅜" tip hang over.

4. Set seam with **Diamond** on top.

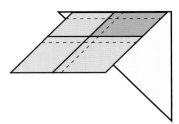

5. Open, and press toward **Diamond**. Trim tip.

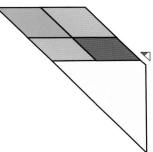

6. Place with Small Triangles.

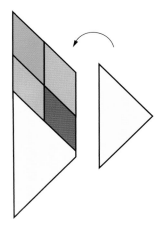

7. Flip Small Triangle right sides together to patch. Let ⅜" tip hang over on top edge.

8. Assembly-line sew.

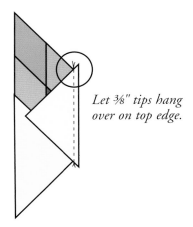

Let ⅜" tips hang over on top edge.

9. Set seam with Diamond on top.

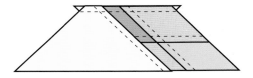

10. Open, and press toward Diamond. Trim tips. Straighten edge if necessary with 6" x 12" Ruler.

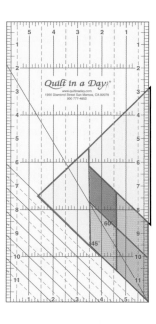

Sewing Left Half

1. Lay out left half.

2. Flip Diamond right sides together to Small Triangle on left.

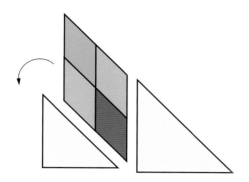

3. Let ⅜" tip hang over on top edge. Assembly-line sew.

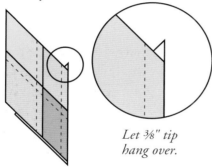

Let ⅜" tip hang over.

4. Set seam with **Small Triangle** on top.

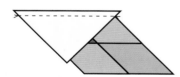

5. Open, and press toward Small Triangle. Using ruler as a straight edge, trim tips.

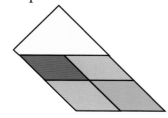

6. Place with **Large Triangles.**

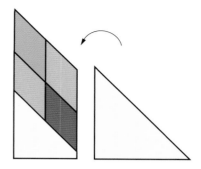

7. Flip Large Triangle right sides together to patch. Let ⅜" tip hang over on top edge. Line up on bottom edge.

8. Assembly-line sew.

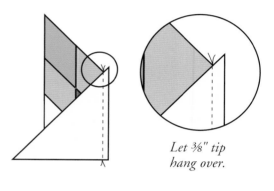

Let ⅜" tip hang over.

9. For locking seams, set seam with **Large Triangle** on top.

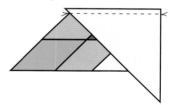

10. Open, and press toward Large Triangle. Trim tip. Straighten edges using 45° line on ruler as your guide.

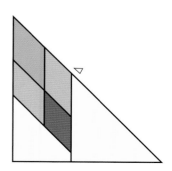

Sewing Quarters Together

 Sewing Block Together

1. Lay out Left and Right patches.

1. Lay out four patches. Carefully match Star seams. **Outside edges may be uneven.**

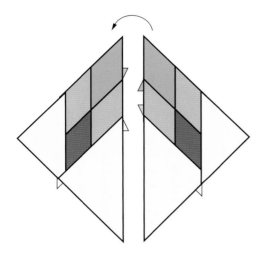

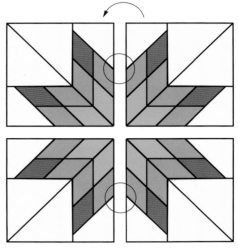

Straighten inside edges.

2. Flip right sides together. Lock Diamonds. Match and pin Diamond seams and ends together. Sew.

2. Flip vertical row of patches on right to vertical row of patches on left, right sides together. Put needle in fabric and presser foot down to avoid jamming. Start out sewing slowly.

3. Lock seams, and assembly-line sew. Do not clip connecting thread.

4. Turn. Flip vertical row on right to vertical row on left.

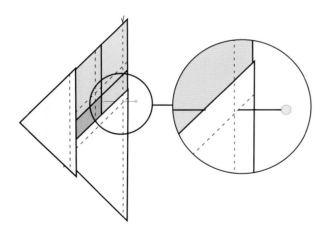

3. Set seam with stitches across top, open, and press.

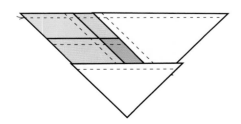

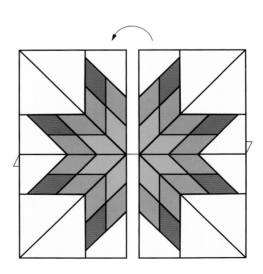

5. Lock center seams, pushing top seam up, and underneath seam down.

6. Sew.

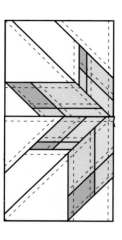

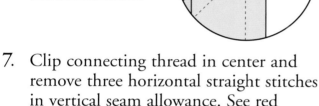

7. Clip connecting thread in center and remove three horizontal straight stitches in vertical seam allowance. See red thread.

8. Turn block over and remove remaining three straight stitches.

9. Place on pressing mat wrong side up. Push top vertical seam to right, and bottom vertical seam to left. Center will pop open and make a little pinwheel.

10. Press center flat with your finger. Press so seams swirl around center clockwise.

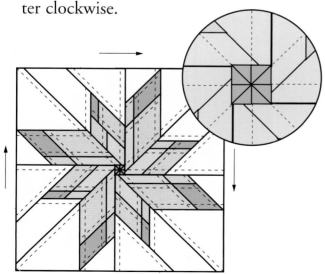

Squaring Little Stars for Four and Six Color Radiant Stars

1. Place block on cutting mat.

2. Square block to 10½" with 12½" Square Up Ruler.

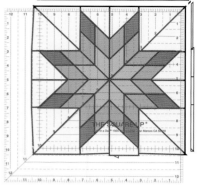

Place 5¼" lines on one quarter of block. Trim right and top sides.

Turn block. Do not turn ruler. Place 10½" lines on just cut edges.

Trim right and top edges.

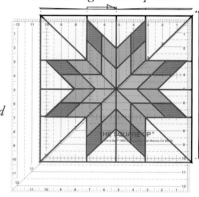

Squaring Little Stars for Seven Color Radiant Stars

1. Place block on cutting mat.

2. Square block to 15" with 16" Square Up Ruler.

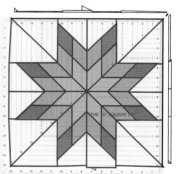

Place 7½" lines on one quarter of block. Trim right and top sides.

Turn block. Do not turn ruler. Place 15" lines on just cut edges. Trim right and top edges.

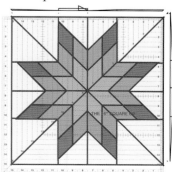

Framing Little Stars for Four and Seven Color Radiant Stars

1. Cut eight 1½" (3½") strips same size as Stars.

2. Sew strips to each side of Star.

3. Set seams with strips on top, open, and press seams toward strips.

4. Measure. Cut eight strips same size.

5. Sew strips to top and bottom.

6. Set seams with strips on top, open, and press seams toward strips.

7. Square blocks to size of Corner Squares. See pages 60 – 62.

8. Sew Little Stars into Corners in place of one piece Corner Squares.

Framing Little Stars for Six Color Radiant Stars

1. Cut eight Background 10½" squares on one diagonal.

2. Fold Triangles in half and make a crease.

3. Place Triangles on opposite sides of Star. Match centers, and pin.

4. Sew with triangles on bottom.

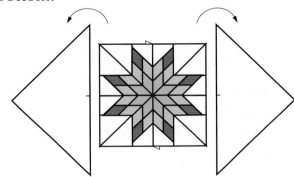

5. Press with triangles on top, open, and press toward triangles. Trim triangles even with blocks

6. Place remaining two triangles on opposite side. Pin and sew with triangles on bottom.

7. Open and press.

8. Square blocks to size of Corner Squares. See pages 60 – 62.

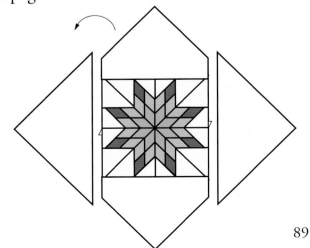

Sassy Stars

These 10" scrappy stars are made from one coordinated Honey Bun. Divide your strips into groups of three colors.

 Select one strip from one color for Center A.

 Select two of the same color for Radiant B.

 Select one strip from last color for Points C.

Each grouping of four strips will yield two stars. If you double your yardage, you can make two quilts.

Sue Bouchard
Amie Potter
60" x 60"

Sassy Stars 60" x 60"

One Honey Bun or Thirty-six 1½" strips

Make nine different Star blocks following directions beginning on page 80 for 10" Little Stars.

Background	1¾ yds
Stars	(3) 3½" strips cut into (36) 3½" squares
	(4) 4¼" strips cut into (36) 4¼" squares
Lattice	(6) 1½" strips
Nine-Patch Cornerstones	(5) 1½" strips
First Border	(5) 2½" strips
Medium	**¾ yd**
Lattice	(12) 1½" strips
Nine-Patch Cornerstones	(4) 1½" strips
Second Border	**1⅓ yds**
	(6) 7" strips
Bias Binding	1 yd
Backing	3¾ yds
Batting	68" x 68"

Optional: For Scallop Edge, use Quilt in a Day's Scallop, Vines & Waves Template and Bias Stripper for 2¼" Bias Binding. Instructions are included with the products.

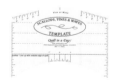

Scallops, Vines & Waves Template

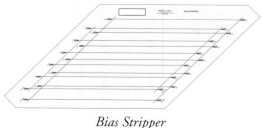

Bias Stripper

Making Sixteen Nine-Patches

1. Place 1½" strips in order.

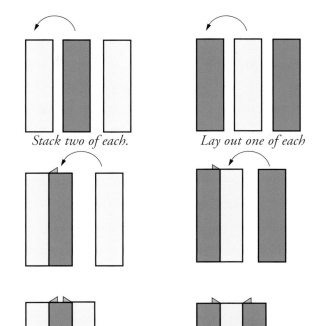

Stack two of each. *Lay out one of each*

2. Assembly-line sew strips together.

3. Press seams toward medium.

4. Place strips on cutting mat. Square left end with 6" Square Up Ruler.

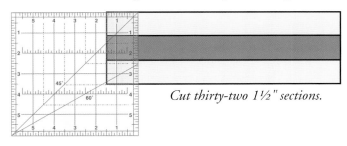

Cut thirty-two 1½" sections.

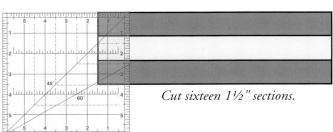

Cut sixteen 1½" sections.

5. Cut thirty-two Light/Medium/Light 1½" sections.

6. Cut sixteen Medium/Light/Medium 1½" sections.

7. Sew sixteen Nine-Patches together.

8. Press last seam toward center.

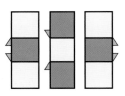 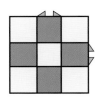

Sewing Lattice Strips

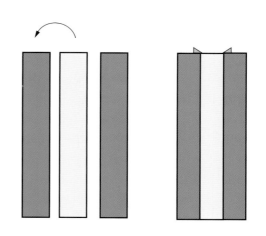

1. Place six 1½" selvage to selvage strips in each stack.

2. Assembly-line sew strips.

3. Press seams toward medium.

4. Cut twenty-four 10½" sections.

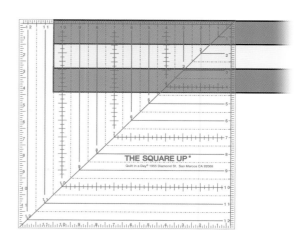

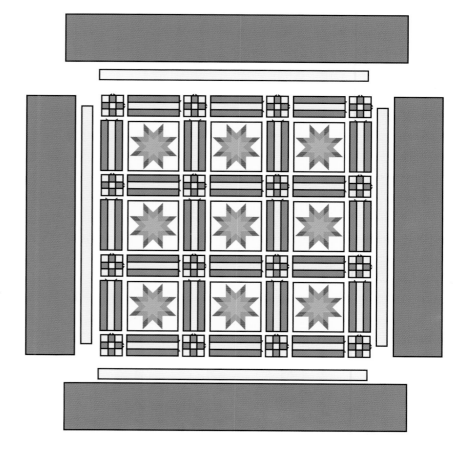

5. Lay out Star blocks with Lattice and Cornerstones.

6. Sew top together.

7. Press seams toward Lattice.

Marking and Sewing Scallops

1. Follow directions with Quilt in a Day's Scallop, Vines & Waves Template.

2. Cut 2¼" bias strips with Quilt in a Day's Bias Stripper.

3. Layer, quilt, and bind.

Grandma's Star

Teresa's old fashioned quilt is charming out of reproduction 1930's fabrics. For her Seven Color Star, Teresa cut scrappy selvage to selvage 2½" strips totaling the number of strips needed for each of seven fabrics. (Page 21) When she finished her traditional 15" Corner Stars from 2" strips and had leftovers, her bright idea of sewing half Stars and framing them with 3½" strips completed her masterpiece!

Side Triangle Half Star

Grandma's Star
Teresa Varnes
Amie Potter
88" x 88"

Amie never ceases to amaze!
Here she sparkled with imagination
using feathers, loops, and hearts assuring
this quilt is over the moon gorgeous.

93

Index

Paradise Star
Teresa Varnes
Amie Potter
48" x 48"

Teresa chose her inspiration fabric with a beach motif. It was easy to pick the colors of sand and tranquil waters to carry out her theme. Amie spread the radiance with straight quilting bursting from the quilt's angles.

Acknowledgements

Thanks to our stars! Your quilts shine!

Quilt Piecers

Sue Bouchard

Angela Castro

Julie Ferrick

Carol Frey

Robin Kinley

Patricia Knoechel

Karyn Helsel

Martha Quintero

Lenore Ryden

Teresa Varnes

Patty Wood

Gail Yakos

Long Arm Quilters

Judy Jackson

Robin Kinley

Amie Potter

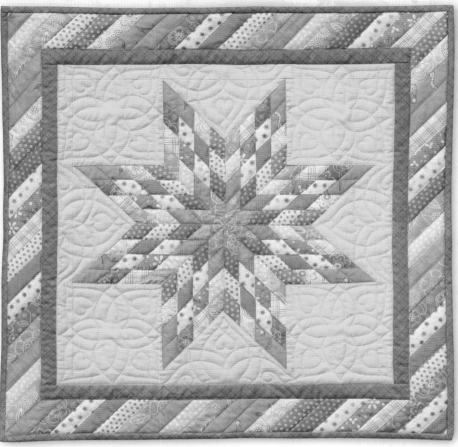

Sunny Skies
Sue Bouchard
Amie Potter
28" x 28"

Pieced with only one Honey Bun for her Star, Sue's diamonds are only 1" finished! This small Wallhanging is sure to brighten up any wall. Sue also designed an innovative border treatment by cutting her leftover strip sets into 3½" wide pieces. Amie placed a Celtic style motif in the background and stitched in the ditch throughout the pieced stripe border.

Order Information

Quilt in a Day books offer a wide range of techniques and are directed toward a variety of skill levels. If you do not have a quilt shop in your area, you may write or call for a complete catalog and current price list of all books and patterns published by Quilt in a Day®, Inc. Check out our website for books, rulers, and current events.

Quilt in a Day
1955 Diamond St.
San Marcos, CA 92078
800 777-4852
www.quiltinaday.com

Martha loves intense colors and a challenge! As a beginning quilter, she dove fearlessly into her Radiant Star project with rare confidence. She had never touched a pattern this difficult. Using the Bias Stripper and the Set In Triangle ruler took all the intimidation out of it for her and she finished her Star in record time. Amie used continuous curves for the Star and continuous tulip shapes for the background and yellow inside border.

Intensity
Martha Quintero
Amie Potter
82" x 82"